MASTERING
THE CUBE

*Overcoming Stumbling Blocks and
Building an Organization that Works*

REED DESHLER, KREIG SMITH, AND ALYSON VON FELDT

A Leader's Guide to Orchestrating Complex Organizational Change

Editor's note: Some of the names and identifying information in this book have been changed to protect the privacy of those involved.

Library of Congress Control Number: 2014941065

ISBNs:
978-0-9903854-3-1 (hardcover)
978-0-9903854-4-8 (paperback)
978-0-9903854-5-5 (ebook)

Any Internet references contained in this work are current at publication time, but the publisher cannot guarantee that a specific location will continue to be maintained.

Published by AlignOrg Solutions

For our spouses Heather, Sherry, and Doug and our families, who, in the end, comprise the greatest work we shall ever do on this earth.

ACKNOWLEDGEMENTS

We appreciate the continuous learning culture of our AlignOrg Solutions team, who find creative ways to address tough organizational challenges each day with our clients and inspire us to constantly innovate. Many of the ideas in this book have been enriched by their contributions.

Special thanks to Adam Anderson and Max Hobbs who helped develop the central metaphor of this book, gave countless hours to fine-tuning the word choice of our stumbling and building blocks, and provided insightful feedback on multiple versions of the manuscript. Max carefully oversaw the visual design of the book. Thanks also to Ken Brophy, Mike Smith, Lorin Walker, Mark Rhodes, Janice Schonwetter, Bridie Fanning, and Doug Von Feldt, who also made notable contributions to the content.

Finally, we thank our clients, especially those who appear in the book's case studies (disguised in most instances), for their wisdom and valor as alignment leaders.

CONTENTS

ALIGNMENT AND THE MULTIFACETED ORGANIZATION

We humans have a brilliant ability to organize ourselves into groups and plan out how to get our work done. We have evolved to collaborate. We love it. We crave it. We cannot live without it, quite literally.

As a result, the world we live in today is filled with the largest and most complex organizations ever known—organizations that span markets, channels, disciplines, functions, and even industries and continents. We have outdone ourselves.

Coordination, collaboration, and change in these organizations are exquisite challenges. In the past few decades, we have benefitted from spectacularly innovative technologies that make coordination easier than in the past. Yet—or therefore—organizations continually grow more complex and the demands on leaders become ever more challenging.

The leader of a large department, division, corporation, government entity, or nonprofit organization stands at the pinnacle of this complexity. When the enterprise strategy changes, when growth is mandated, or when marketplace performance must be stimulated, it falls on the leader to spearhead organization changes that will deliver new results.

Indeed, leaders at all levels are responsible for effecting change no matter where they fit in the complex organizational ecosystem.

This is an incredibly daunting responsibility given the enormous stakes. Billions of dollars (or yuan or euros or yen) may be at risk, as well as thousands of livelihoods, the world's intricately interconnected marketplaces, and the limited resources of our precious planet.

The message of this book is that no matter how large the organization or how significant the strategic changes required, *the only way leaders will generate sustainable enhancements to organizational performance is by ensuring that the elements of their organization are optimally aligned to the enterprise strategy.*

Let's consider the experience of one business leader, Peter Sun, as he faced significant organizational change. At the launch of a major realignment of a marketing business to deliver a new, more sophisticated, experience-driven strategy, Sun presented what we thought was a superb analogy. "This is going to be like solving a Rubik's Cube," he told his team. "When you look at one of the sides of the cube and start making changes, it's going to scramble all of the other colors."

Sun saw the organization as a giant Rubik's Cube and his role as the alignment leader responsible for getting all the sides composed correctly. His analogy was meant to prime his team to take a comprehensive, multifaceted approach to organizational design—an effort that would require them to view the organization not as divisions and departments but as an integrated, complete system. Finding the right configuration would demand patience and tenacity. At times, they would develop a distinctive new process but it would be impossible to execute without modifying the interactions among departments. Redrawing the organization chart might bring focus to new marketing priorities but at the same time break crucial links for maintaining strong product knowledge. The team might feel like maddened Rubik's Cube novices, trying to hit upon the one successful alignment among literally 43 quintillion flops.

It may not be surprising to learn that the Hungarian inventor of the Rubik's Cube, Erno Rubik, was educated as an architect and was fascinated with puzzles. He designed the Rubik's Cube when he became absorbed with the problem of connecting small blocks together so they could move independently without falling apart.[1] That is also what an alignment leader does—finds ways to connect the moving pieces of an organization so they can work together in a flexible yet unified way.

Michael D. Watkins, in a June 2012 *Harvard Business Review* article titled "How Managers Become Leaders," discusses the importance of becoming an organization architect, or what we're calling an *alignment leader*. He writes that leaders "must become responsible for designing and altering the architecture of their organization—its strategy, structure, processes, and skill bases. To be effective architects, they must think in terms of systems. They must understand how the key elements of the organization fit together and not naïvely believe . . . that they can alter one element without thinking through the implications for all the others."[2] They cannot twist one side of the cube without affecting the other sides.

Our belief is that all enterprise leaders should consider themselves alignment leaders along with the other roles they play. Chief executives should know that their duties include serving as the Chief Alignment Officer (CAO). Because chief executives are ultimately responsible for product, profits, and people, they must also attend to the health and effectiveness of the very organizations that deliver these benefits for their constituents.

Leaders can do this more effectively when they realize that the organization is like a complex Rubik's Cube and the puzzle is solved—the game is won—by adjusting the blocks so that the colors on all of the sides are aligned. Alignment leaders make choices about how to reposition, redesign, or retool each of the organization's many facets until they can effectively work together to deliver the strategy. Organizing choices drive results. Organizing choices based on sound principles and aligned together lead to marketplace wins.

Of course, people throughout an organization are always making organizing choices and impacting strategy. It is not just the leader who does it. New products are being developed. New practices are being put in place. New relationships are being forged. While all this brilliant collaboration is going on, an insightful leader must be watchful to ensure that the various efforts are harmonized to impact the overall strategy in a positive way rather than to optimize the well-intentioned but sometimes misaligned smaller goals of a certain function, subsystem, or individual agenda.

Much has been written about the leader's role in imagining and articulating the enterprise vision, in developing strategies and communicating them simply and forcefully. Less has been said about how to constantly build, rebuild, and coordinate all of the work processes and hierarchies inherent in a complex organization to realize those strategies. This is what alignment leaders think about. *Alignment leaders are passionate about optimal organization alignment to strategy.*

Most business leaders hold this ideal, but it can be difficult to pull off. In the absence of adequate insight about how to coordinate design choices throughout an enterprise, leaders sometimes come to rely on faulty practices or myths they have observed throughout their careers. In this book, we identify eight such stumbling blocks that we have seen repeatedly. While some of these practices can result in small missteps with little consequence, others can inflict real damage to the organization, destroy the bottom line, and land leaders flat on their faces.

For example, many executives begin redrawing an organization chart when they are not seeing adequate focus on a given product, customer group, territory, channel, or other concern. It seems reasonable that changing reporting relationships would promote a new emphasis in some areas and demote groups that play a role less critical to strategic success. But relying on structural change without considering the implications across the organization is like trying to solve only one side of the Rubik's Cube. Toward the overall goal of winning the game, such a move is almost always inadequate and may even be harmful. Important connections may be unintentionally broken by new reporting relationships. New measures may be required to gauge the success of new groups. Decision-making rights may need to be renegotiated.

Like a kid on Christmas morning, uninformed organization aligners (alignment leaders) may somehow luck into solving a Rubik's Cube but will more likely scramble the puzzle even further. As Watkins wrote, "Too often, senior executives dabble in the profession of organizational design without a license—and end up committing malpractice." They "target elements of the organization that seem relatively easy to change, like strategy or structure, without completely understanding the effect their moves will have on the organization as a whole."[3] Their efforts can replace the existing disarray with a new set of problems, or even worse, jumble an organization into utter chaos. Hoping for a big payoff, these leaders are disappointed when results don't show any improvement.

In this book, we will explore the 8 Stumbling Blocks that we see most often in our consulting practice. These are misguided moves intended to address common considerations that alignment leaders weigh as they embark on change, but they do not result in systemic alignment or improved marketplace success. They are beliefs about how to make organizing choices that are intended to improve the bottom line, but in reality only cause pain without any gain. Unexamined, they will continue to trip up leaders and slow or even halt progress.

To avoid these stumbling blocks, leaders need sound techniques to accomplish their marketplace goals. So for each stumbling block, we offer a countering building block—a solid principle or method for leading organization alignment. By replacing the 8 Stumbling Blocks with 8 Building Blocks, business leaders can more effectively design their way to a winning organization. The overarching secret is optimal system alignment to strategy.

Below is a synopsis of the 8 Stumbling Blocks and 8 Building Blocks that we will detail in this book, showing you just how to avoid falling into these common traps and instead take action that will create a fully aligned organization:

For Approaching Structural Change

Stumbling Block 1: Boxology. This is the belief that redrawing the boxes on the organization chart is the secret to better results. Structure change is the only card that some leaders ever play in the role of lead organization aligner. But that is like trying to achieve a uniform color on only one face of a Rubik's Cube while ignoring the kaleidoscope that is the rest of the system.

Building Block 1: Align All Systems. Effective organization alignment considers all the facets of the enterprise, and it ensures that your strategy, capabilities, and choices work together to generate the results you desire.

For Designing the Right Organization

Stumbling Block 2: Off-the-Shelf Organizations. This is tackling organization structure change as if it were a multiple-choice question. It's false to assume there is a small set of templates to choose from to get the organization chart right.

Building Block 2: Tailor to Strategy. Your organization's structure should be as unique as your organization's strategy and should be informed by that strategy. Furthermore, the other organization elements with which the structure is enmeshed should be tailored to your strategy as well. Strategic teams can work together to clarify strategic direction and strategic trade-offs, then embed these decisions deep in the design of the organization.

For Choosing Who to Involve in the Alignment Process

Stumbling Block 3: The Secret Society. This is the misguided belief that organization alignment is the covert work of a select few. You see it in action when leaders seclude themselves in a conference room on Friday afternoon and then announce the new organization chart on Monday morning. Omitting the broader expertise of top directors, managers, and other experts will not only result in faulty organization alignment but will also lead to slower and less effective implementation of the plan.

Building Block 3: Co-create. The more people who are involved in alignment deliberations, the more likely it is that the effort will generate substantial organization and behavioral change. The benefits of widespread involvement clearly outweigh the downsides.

For When to Select the Right People for New Jobs

Stumbling Block 4: Starting with Names. Leaders who start with the skills and abilities of their most valued associates and build an organization from there have encountered this pitfall. They may align their organizations to their people, but they won't necessarily create alignment between their organization and their strategy.

Building Block 4: Staffing Follows Structure. It's better to align individual strengths to strategy as embodied in the new structure. You might have to wait for the organization alignment process to unfold before you can determine who will fit where, but when you patiently fill roles with people who possess the right skills and abilities for the new jobs, you enable the new structure to reach its full potential.

For How to Lead to Alignment

Stumbling Block 5: "Real" Work. Speeding through organization alignment in order to get on with "real" work is a major stumble. When organization alignment efforts are viewed as a distraction from what actually makes an organization hum, it is clear that the leader has not yet recognized that one of his or her most critical roles is that of alignment leader.

Building Block 5: Become an Alignment Leader. Alignment leaders know that organization design is a process to solve problems and that bringing other people along to think about alignment generates enormous power for the organization. We will describe the distinct set of characteristics that define an alignment leader.

For How to Accomplish Goals using Alignment

*Stumbling Block 6: Grow **or** Cut.* This is the false belief that a business can either increase revenues or shrink expenses, but not both at the same time.

*Building Block 6: Resource **and** Reduce.* Alignment leaders don't despair when they are faced with both growth and savings targets simultaneously. They know it is possible to have it all—and they know how to protect and cut work strategically.

For Embracing Simplicity and Complexity

Stumbling Block 7: The Simplicity Complex. There is a lot of talk about how much consumers want simplicity in the form of elegantly integrated products and customized solutions. But most existing organizations are not built for these new kinds of offerings, and they may not realize how much re-architecting is called for. They make the mistake of adapting their strategy without adapting their own organization.

Building Block 7: Absorb Complexity. Organizations that choose to absorb complexity for their customers are prepared to develop new capabilities, and they know that these new capabilities will require them to make some trade-offs.

For Knowing When to Align

Stumbling Block 8: One and Done. Complete alignment of an organization can feel like a massive undertaking. Consequently, there is a tendency to want to create the perfect organization design once and for all. Leaders who are out to create a flawless new organization in one fell swoop are setting themselves up for disappointment.

Building Block 8: Design Fluidly. A better mindset is to be continuously remaking the organization to track new marketplace conditions and the resulting strategic adjustments. Designing fluidly means moving smoothly and constantly to tweak organization alignment.

Now of course we cannot provide formulas for aligning a complex organization that leaders can learn by rote and execute without customization, but we think there are systematic ways of approaching the alignment problems that leaders face, and these are encompassed in the 8 Building Blocks. We have seen these approaches work consistently in companies, governments, and nonprofits of all sizes and types around the world. If you build your approach on these methods, you can feel confident that your organization alignment efforts will result in real change.

What Does It Mean to Master the Cube?

The cube we have in mind when we use the title metaphor of this book is the multifaceted organization in its entirety—all of its strategies, processes, structures, systems, practices, and metrics, as well as the skills, values, and beliefs of its people. Mastering this cube means knowing the most effective techniques for approaching and orchestrating complex organization change so that all of these components come into alignment. It means thinking systemically, anticipating both the desirable outcomes that will result from a design choice as well as the reverberations likely to be felt in other parts of the enterprise. The word "master" connotes the ability to direct or perform something skillfully. If you know how to master an organization, you are skilled at orchestrating all its disparate parts so they work well together. An expert alignment leader is a master of the organizational cube.

To help you become a master of the cube, we demonstrate in each chapter how the 8 Stumbling Blocks and 8 Building Blocks often play out in real-life situations. We present a list of key concepts for leading successful organization alignment efforts, which we add to as the book proceeds and consolidate at the end. We wrap up each chapter with a set of questions to consider as you apply what you have learned in your own work. Along the way we offer some alignment aphorisms that together with the building blocks condense some of the most important ideas. We gather these in the last chapter as well.

The happy truth is that a surprisingly simple series of discussions can help leaders of even very large and intricate organizations create an enterprise that is aligned, top to bottom, to the singular goals of the enterprise strategy, one that is adept at continually and quickly re-creating itself in our ever-changing world. Such an approach makes organization innovation much more likely—people developing novel organizations that give them an advantage in their realm.

Organization alignment needs neither to be overwhelming nor naïve. Nor should it be a singular endeavor, an all-out, distasteful, stop-the-machines upheaval. Rather, every leader should become familiar with positive practices based on solid building blocks for aligning an organization and keeping it aligned. It is one of the most crucial skills needed in commerce, in government, and in nonprofit organizations today.

What You Can Do Now

This book is meant for alignment leaders; that is, executives and others responsible for making organizing choices to see their companies, foundations, institutions, communities, or other groups to success. It is also meant for those who support and facilitate organization alignment work, such as partners and other practitioners in human resources, organization effectiveness, organization design, strategy, information technology, and process or continuous improvement (e.g., Lean Six Sigma). We will refer to all of these roles as *change partners*. Because, as we will argue, organization alignment should be an interactive process, both the executive role and the partner role are essential. One cannot delegate all the responsibilities for organization alignment to the other.

The most beneficial way for any reader to use this book is to bear in mind an organization alignment challenge that is before you now. Sometimes these situations arise due to business performance issues; other times they surface when you aspire to build an institution that is even better than it is today. Either way, we suggest that you select a situation that is tough, that is multifaceted and will require the action of multiple levers, and that may impact the thinking of many people in your organization.

At the end of each chapter, we present specific questions and applications to help you personally use the building blocks highlighted in this book. We also encourage you to invite your organization alignment partners (your change partners) to read this book as well, then share your thoughts and notes from the end of each chapter. Discuss the truths and positive practices you can use to rise to the challenge of your specific situation. Discuss how you can work together to meet your common goals.

To get started with your exploration, answer the questions that apply to your role.

If you are an alignment leader:

- What business challenge are you currently facing that seems to lie just beyond or under the surface of the obvious fixes or solutions?
- What would your organization be like in the future if you were able to effectively address this challenge?
- What are the consequences now and in the long-term if you are not able to handle this challenge?
- What have you tried so far? What has worked? What has not worked?

If you are a change partner:

- What organizational challenges do you see your organization struggling with? Think of issues that seem too complex or too sensitive to address.
- What do leaders seem most concerned about solving?
- What would be the consequences now and in the long-term if the organization were not able to effectively address these challenges?
- What have you tried so far to either address these challenges yourself or to partner with a leader in the organization to tackle these challenges?

For both alignment leaders and change partners:

- Have you spoken to the other about your thoughts and concerns?
- What plans or approaches have you jointly been able to conceive for addressing these challenges?

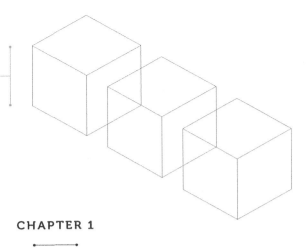

CHAPTER 1

HOW TO APPROACH STRUCTURAL CHANGE

When Ernest Jimenez assumed the leadership role for the growth markets of an international security service and systems provider, he had already led operational and financial turnarounds all over the world as well as the integration of significant acquisitions. His imperative was to more than triple one of the firm's core businesses in Latin America, southern Africa, the Middle East, and India in five years. Jimenez was no neophyte, but this challenge was his biggest yet.

In one Middle Eastern market, Jimenez could see a number of operational problems, but before launching reforms, he took steps to clarify the strategy. Though the residential market for subscription security services was nearly saturated in this country, the commercial market was underplayed. His team set a 90 percent growth target over three years, the majority of which was to be generated through the commercial sector. But company leaders in the country had already been trying to penetrate the commercial market; they had eagerly launched the effort and created new commercial sales jobs to really go after commercial customers. Results had not delivered the kind of growth Jimenez's team was envisioning.

With this new information in hand, Jimenez could see that the business needed to be significantly realigned.

● BOXOLOGY
STUMBLING BLOCK 1

Even when the challenges are not as hefty as those faced by Jimenez, many new leaders of large organizations or divisions select restructuring as their first move to begin an organization turnaround. When an enterprise faces serious problems because its business results are unacceptable, or when it faces daunting new growth or revenue challenges, conventional wisdom says to get out the organization charts and start rearranging the boxes.

Most executives and analysts know the business school axiom "structure follows strategy"—that is, changing a company's strategy often necessitates a change in its structure. Since structure follows strategy, an announcement of imminent structural change often signals that a remade strategy is being deployed.

It's true that restructuring is a highly visible and speedy way for a new leader to make a move. It is decisive and action-oriented. In cases where a business has been steadily underperforming, a leader's announcement that she has launched a restructure can be reassuring to board members and investors. It implies that the right steps—bold steps—are under way to address problems or achieve new heights.

But we offer this warning: a new structure does not always indicate a substantial change in strategy. Structure only enables strategy; it can never drive it. In fact, a new structure can be *mistaken* for a new strategy. For example, the boxes on the organization chart can be reduced or rearranged simply to cut costs with no real vision about how to gain additional revenues or to protect the work or groups that provide the greatest value in terms of customer satisfaction and profitability.

Nor is a restructure by itself enough to change results, even if the strategy has been adjusted thoughtfully. Done in isolation, structure changes can scramble the other five sides of the cube and create more problems than they resolve.

Expecting too much from the structure of an organization is Stumbling Block 1. It almost always is a mistake. Structure enables strategy but in and of itself is generally not sufficient for effecting lasting change and improvement.

Think of your own experience. How many times have you undergone restructuring efforts that did not change any strategic capabilities or ultimately any results? Most executives have experienced dozens of restructurings, but when we ask them how many of these brought about changes to organization capability or improvements to the bottom line, the answer is very few.

If this is the collective experience of leaders, why do they continually place so much faith in restructuring?

The misguided reliance on restructuring in isolation of change to other organization systems is sometimes ironically referred to as *boxology*. Boxology is the attempt to transmute an unsatisfactory organization into a thriving one by diligently reshuffling the boxes of the organizational chart, layering them or consolidating them into a new and more perfect configuration, then filling them with the right people to lead the organization into its new age.

Rearranging the boxes in the organizational chart without considering other strategic or operational improvements is not enough to turn around a company or elevate it to the next level of performance. There is no one structure that alone will produce organization perfection. Nor in most cases will appointing a new leader or two to fill new positions be adequate to produce change without also addressing underlying systemic issues, no matter how extraordinary those leaders are.

ALIGN ALL SYSTEMS
BUILDING BLOCK 1

In contrast to the mythical science of boxology, the leadership discipline of *organization alignment* reaches far beyond questions of structure and organizational charts. Effective organization alignment is an approach leaders use to translate the requirements of the external environment into strategy and into an organization that can deliver that strategy, which requires examining all the sides of the cube. *Align all systems to strategy is Building Block 1.*

Here is what organization alignment is all about: clarifying the value you offer that is different from that of any other organization (strategy), determining what you need to be good at doing differently from others to deliver that offering (capabilities), and making a thoughtful set of choices all aligned toward developing and delivering those capabilities (choices).

Figure 1.1: Elements of Organization Alignment

Strategy

An aligned organization is impossible to achieve if the strategy is not clear, because strategy is the endpoint to which the rest of the organization is directed. When leaders set about to align their organizations, they often discover that they are not resolved about their strategy. They may be very clear about their financial targets. They may have precise numbers representing their growth plans. They may be sure of the capital initiatives and other initiatives they have planned to pursue in the short- or long-term. But if your team cannot exactly articulate why customers choose you over others—or in the case of nonprofit organizations, what your beneficiaries rely on you to do that no one else does for them—then you are not yet capable of alignment. Everyone on the executive team and beyond should be able to state in explicit terms how you intend to be unique in customers' eyes.

Hand in hand with the exercise of precisely articulating your differentiated offering goes the exercise of precisely articulating what you knowingly and happily choose *not* to offer. These are your trade-offs. If you are Netflix, you do not build retail stores to rent or retrieve a movie or game. If you are RyanAir, you trade off reserved seats and customer service processes.

Strategic alignment demands strategic trade-offs.

Restructuring often becomes a cloak that hides the need for trade-offs concerning resource allocation, decision rights, and interdepartmental linkages—in short, the alignment of a diverse set of choices. Since restructuring does not by itself create capabilities, when restructuring is the method relied on to be the workhorse of organization change, it actually can preclude actions that would have a real bottom line impact.

An example of an organization with clearly defined strategy and trade-offs is Starbucks, the chain so successful in America. They differentiate themselves by offering excellent and innovative coffee beverages, by serving them in convenient locations, and by cultivating an inviting, friendly atmosphere in their stores (among other things). Their trade-offs include higher staffing costs, higher prices, and a higher supply chain cost because they control purchasing, roasting, packaging, and distribution.

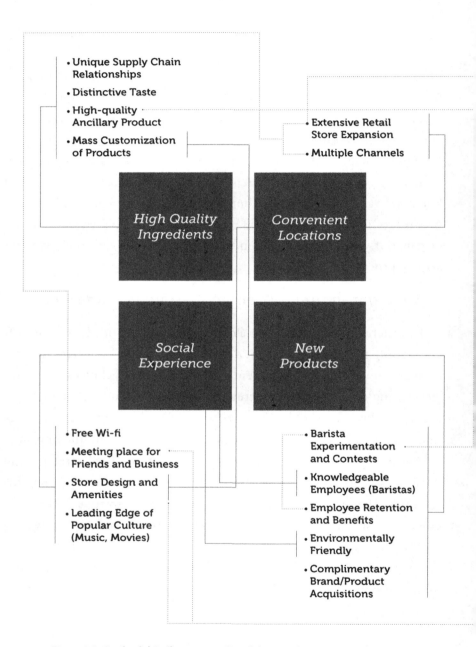

Figure 1.2: Starbucks' Differentiating Capabilities and Organizing Choices.
(Activity map concept adapted from Michael E. Porter, "What Is Strategy?"
Harvard Business Review, November–December 1996, 61–78.)

Capabilities

When you change your strategy, it is likely that the organization as a whole or in part will need to develop new capabilities. A *strategic capability* (which we will mostly refer to as a *capability*) is simply the power and ability to deploy a strategy; a capability is made up of dozens of processes, structures, systems, human resource practices, skilled people, and values interacting throughout an organization. For example, if you are Netflix and you are going to offer media streaming services in addition to DVD rentals, you will need new capabilities in technology, marketing, pricing, vendor management, customer service, and much more.

Let's continue building on the Starbucks example. Their strategy requires capabilities in obtaining high-quality ingredients, selecting convenient locations for their stores and outlets, creating a pleasing social climate in their stores, and developing innovative new products (among other things). These capabilities are represented by the dark squares in figure 1.2. The bulleted text shows the network of individual organizing choices that come together to create the strategic capabilities.

Each needed capability will be developed as you make choices such as establishing groups to perform new work, creating new processes, developing new jobs, forming new vendor relationships, and gauging your progress with new measures. When you have a unique set of aligned organizing choices that allows you to be recognizably different from your competitors, what you have is a *differentiating capability* (fig. 1.3). And that is what you want.

Figure 1.3: Alignment for Differentiation.

Declaring your strategy is about the future: this is how we will win; this is how we will differentiate ourselves; this is what we will offer; this is what we will *not* offer. As soon as you declare a new strategy for the future, the organization is already behind because its current capabilities are aligned to the past strategy.

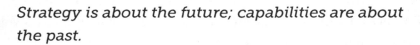

Strategy is about the future; capabilities are about the past.

Understanding the delta between your current capabilities and the needed capabilities is the crux of organization alignment.

You need to select which existing capabilities will be augmented and which will be attenuated or discontinued altogether. Developing new capabilities takes time, and backing off from old capabilities takes courage.

Choices

Organizations need differentiating capabilities to execute differentiating strategy. Capabilities can only be differentiating when the mix of organizing choices is also aligned in a differentiating way. Leaders develop new, distinctive capabilities in their organizations through the choices they make in six categories or *organization systems*: (1) work processes, (2) structure and governance, (3) information and metrics, (4) people and rewards, (5) continuous improvement, and (6) leadership and culture (fig. 1.4). These organization systems operate as the six sides of the organizational Rubik's Cube, and they must be aligned to the strategy.

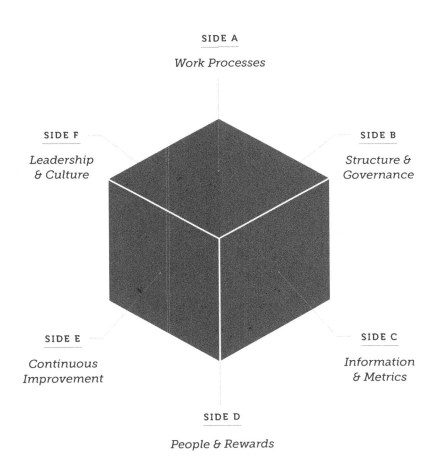

SIDE A

Work Processes

SIDE F

*Leadership
& Culture*

SIDE B

*Structure &
Governance*

SIDE E

*Continuous
Improvement*

SIDE C

*Information
& Metrics*

SIDE D

People & Rewards

Figure 1.4: Organizing Systems and Choices

Side A: Work Processes

At the very heart of an organization are the tasks that employees perform every day to create and deliver value. This is where an organization competes: down deep in the guts of routines and processes. If organization alignment efforts do not result in a change in work activities, leaders should not expect new revenues, new efficiencies, or new customers.

If the work doesn't change, results don't change.

When strategy is adjusted, leadership teams must scrutinize the work of the organization and discern what new or existing activities and touch points will actually deliver differentiation in the marketplace. Not what activities are familiar old friends that have previously contributed to success. Not what activities are headed by the most charismatic or brilliant people in your company. Not what activities are considered "best in class." Not what activities are prescribed by the myriad of institutions that inform the education and professional certification of technical experts you have hired. Not what activities are legislated. Just those activities that will help you win because they set you apart from everyone else.

Differentiating activities deliver competitive differentiation.

Therefore, we call these kinds of activities *competitive work*. It is leaders who must make strategic decisions about the work performed in the organization. They often classify customer-facing work, product innovation, and relationship-building as competitive, but it all depends on the strategy.

Non-competitive work, on the other hand, is work that does not have a competitive upside in the marketplace, even though it may be very important to the functioning of the firm. Compensation, project management, and operational reporting are examples of work that is generally non-competitive (though with certain strategies, leaders may indeed decide to classify this work as competitive).

Continuing the Starbucks example, here are some of the work processes at Starbucks that help generate differentiating capability:

- preparation of "hand-crafted beverages"
- design of stores and their amenities
- selection and establishment of channel relationships for distributing ready-to-drink beverages and other consumer-packaged goods in grocery stores, airports, hotels, schools, restaurants, hospitals, etc.
- hiring, developing, and retaining fast-food workers in a way that is significantly different than standard industry practice

Categorizing work based on its competitive impact helps guide the focus of all efforts to change or improve work activities. Such efforts often fall in the purview of continuous (process) improvement practitioners, many of whom use the methodologies of Lean Six Sigma. These are powerful tools, but they should be wielded with alignment to strategy in mind, because the process improvement goals for competitive work may be very different from the goals for non-competitive work. The aim for competitive work will be to make it as effective as possible, reengineering it if necessary *and possibly spending more* to deliver a better product or customer experience as the strategy directs. The aim for non-competitive work will be to make it as efficient as possible, ensuring it hums along steadily without unnecessarily consuming resources that could be used by work that has a strong marketplace upside.

Your ability to compete lies in the activities you choose to do and how you choose to resource them.

But beware: focusing on the organization's work processes to the exclusion of the other sides of the cube is as much a one-sided approach as is boxology. A dedication to controlling processes can severely stunt the growth of robust strategic capability if it is done in isolation of the strategy or the other organization systems. A number of questions arise at this point: What if the strategic value of each process is never made plain? What if resources are dedicated to improving non-competitive processes while competitive processes languish? What if people with the wrong abilities are performing the processes? What if the wrong information systems are enabling the processes? What if the processes are the wrong processes altogether?

Amazon.com faced just such questions as they began to recover from the stock market crash of 2000. Sales were soaring but their distribution process was struggling. The chief of worldwide operations, Jeff Wilke, asked the question: should Amazon even be in the business of distribution? "Was distribution a commodity or was it a core competency?" he wondered, according to Brad Stone, Jeff Bezos's biographer.[1] Before making the decision to outsource distribution altogether, Wilke gathered leaders, engineers, and academics from across the country at a fulfillment center in Nevada to tackle the question. Bezos himself and members of the team climbed around on the conveyors one day observing how orders moved through the facility. In the end, because Amazon wanted the capability of informing customers when their packages would arrive, the company leaders decided not to outsource distribution at all, nor to purchase better equipment or systems, but to overthrow the prevailing orthodoxies and write their own warehouse picking software. They actually moved toward less automation by using sophisticated algorithms to coordinate the movements of employees picking product from shelves in the fulfillment centers.[2] The result, of course, is Amazon's disruptive capability to ship nearly anything with extraordinary speed and efficiency and to accurately predict when it will arrive.

Try to imagine what would have happened if Amazon had simply found a new vendor for their warehouse software or had outsourced their warehousing and distribution work to save money. Instead, by considering the strategic imperative of this work, the company chose to invest significantly in these processes, so that they came to differentiate Amazon from its competitors and eventually enabled the creation of Amazon Prime.

Though process effectiveness can yield significant savings of precious resources, a leader who habitually relies on process improvement to create strategic change has left an arsenal of tools on the table. A lopsided focus on process can be as much of a stumbling block as a lopsided focus on the organizational chart.

Side B: Structure and Governance

Only after you have identified and assessed the organization's competitive work does it make sense to define a structure that organizes people to come together and deliver the capabilities to fulfill the strategy. For example, companies with a product-driven strategy and competitive work centering on product innovation and marketing, such as P&G (Procter & Gamble), might want to emphasize product expertise by creating divisions that foster deep product knowledge and constant innovation. Service-driven companies, on the other hand, might want to organize by regions in order to provide locally customized offerings because they have determined that meeting local needs is the competitive work of their organization.

Strategy drives work. Work drives structure.

Good structures enable the delivery of capabilities that will distinguish your organization from the competition. They reflect your trade-offs.

Returning to the Starbucks example, the company's organizational structure reflects their strategic priorities:

- Retail divisions are organized by a mixed rationale that groups them *geographically* (U.S. and the Americas; China and Asia Pacific; and Europe, the Middle East, and Africa) and also assigns *channel* responsibility to these groups (Teavana store responsibility is given to the U.S. and Americas division while Channel Development and Emerging Brands responsibility is given to the China and Asia Pacific Division). A *product* focus is given an equivalent strategic emphasis through a Global Coffee group that stewards the coffee category.[3]

- Mobile digital initiatives and product innovation were given top strategic priority when Starbucks created a chief operating officer role in early 2014 to oversee daily retail operations, which had previously reported directly to CEO Howard Shultz. Shultz was then freed to "focus on innovation in coffee, tea and the Starbucks Experience as well as next generation retailing and payments initiatives in the areas of digital, mobile, card, loyalty and e-commerce."[4]

- The growing consumer-packaged segment is enabled by a Global Channel Development Group that brings focus to the Starbucks-branded products distributed at grocery stores and other locations such as Seattle's Best Coffee, Starbucks Via Ready Brew, Tazo Tea, and Evolution Fresh juices and snacks.[5]

Structure—so often mistaken as the single most important aspect of organization design—does not of itself *create* organization capability. Rather, it has a more innocuous role. It either *enables* or *disables* the organization's potential.

Not-for-Profit Organizations

If your organization is not-for-profit, your marketplace is different from the for-profit arena. You may not have any direct competitors. Even so, you still compete for the attention of benefactors and the resources of contributors. You still must give serious thought to how to allocate the resources you have. You must articulate what constituents rely on you to do above the many things that are "nice to do" but not essential to your mission. Your structural decisions will be guided by these priorities.

We often see this truth illustrated in organizations striving to become more customer focused: they decide to redraw functional departments or product divisions into customer segments or departments. New leaders are selected and the new structure announced, but in so many cases, no new customer-focused capabilities ever appear. The structural change may signal the strategic intent of becoming more customer focused, but restructuring alone does not bring forth new day-to-day behaviors, work processes, reward systems, or other results. To achieve a real, lasting focus on the customer, the alignment effort must include the development of new routines, behaviors, and beliefs.

An example is an old and highly respected organization that developed a proprietary technology to extend the life of one of the systems on over-the-road trucks. Their invention not only saved fleet managers huge amounts of money but also provided a significant benefit to the environment by greatly reducing waste. Over the long-term, however, their core service proved inadequate to generate the revenue required by investors, so they made a truck service acquisition to complement their current capabilities. They had high hopes that their more rounded offering would make them the Jiffy Lube of trucks (Jiffy Lube is an international provider of comprehensive auto maintenance services).

The leader of the acquisition team initially took on the role of managing this new business. But more than two years later, he was still running it. It remained an appendage to the organization; it was incorporated only as an arm to the existing organization structure. Its offerings and capabilities were never integrated with the core business. No Jiffy Lube after all.

This is an example of how the structure of the organization *disabled* the new strategy. Though the team succeeded at making a sound acquisition to expand the company's services, the potential synergy of the two organizations was never fully realized because the leaders never found a way to align them into an integrated structure, to create new service packages, or to consolidate back-office work. In this case, the company's leaders most certainly should have rearranged the boxes in the organizational chart to take in the new people and processes! Then together they could have developed new, integrated offerings and realized the strategic advantages of their partnership.

Sides C, D, and E: Information and Metrics; People and Rewards; and Continuous Improvement

The work routines and groups within an enterprise are surrounded and enabled by other organization systems, and it is their interaction as a whole that makes an organization work well. Or not.

There is the information system, including both the measures and data used to run the business as well as the technologies that store, share, and analyze this information.

There is the people and rewards system, which encompasses all the practices involved in recruiting, developing, performance managing, and paying people.

And there are practices regarding continuous improvement, the system that stewards organizational learning and renewal and in so doing keeps an eye on the efficiencies of the other systems. Over time, systems once aligned can become bloated and disjointed from each other. They must be periodically reviewed, revamped, and realigned to again serve the strategy.

Sample choices that help create Starbucks' differentiating capabilities include:

- Information Systems and Metrics:
  - To help differentiate the experience of their store customers, Starbucks developed the technology to offer free and fast Wi-Fi. They were one of the first to accept mobile payments and now more than 10 percent of store purchases are paid through mobile devices.[6]
  - In order to underscore the importance of customer experience rather than financial performance, store metrics are not reported publicly each month.[7]
  - Since part of the strategy is to locate stores conveniently for customers, Starbucks has developed information systems that help employees select store locations based on target demographics.[8]
- People and Rewards: To enable the strategy of hand-crafted beverages and an inviting and friendly atmosphere in stores, extensive training and benefits are provided to the part-time workforce of baristas.[9]

- Continuous Improvement: Customer ideas are solicited through Facebook (over 35 million "likes") and mystarbucksidea.com (which is now inactive, but generated 75,000 suggestions in its first year).[10]

Side F: Leadership and Culture

The final side of the cube, leadership and culture, is more difficult to influence directly than the other five sides. Leaders can have a very direct impact on creating a new process, structure, or performance management system, but it is something else again to create a new culture.

By way of definition, *culture* includes the shared assumptions, beliefs, behaviors, and norms of the workforce. The choices made regarding the other five sides of the cube influence culture and mold beliefs and behaviors. This is why Jeff Bezos, who has long espoused frugality as one of Amazon's core values, provides rudimentary desks made out of doors for his employees and gives them parking subsidies that cover only part of their fees. He hawkishly insists that Amazon leaders live this value as well, so they must all fly coach class, even if they travel frequently. When he brings team members with him in a private jet, he pointedly reminds them that he pays for the jet personally.[11] He knows that Amazon's policies and his team's behaviors must embody the values that the leaders espouse.

Starbucks' leaders seek to promote values and model behaviors that support the strategy of developing an inviting, friendly atmosphere in retail stores, among other things. Here are some examples:

- Example value: "Be personally accountable and responsible for the outcome of every single customer interaction."

- Example behavior: As part of a company turnaround, founder Howard Shultz emphasized the importance of customer service by requiring every store manager to complete five hours of community service. The company organized and funded (to the tune of $1 million) a massive service project to kick off a conference of 10,000 store managers in New Orleans, and leaders, including CEO Shultz, worked alongside store managers as they painted, landscaped, and in other ways restored hard-hit areas of the city after Hurricane Katrina.[12]

Though leadership behavior and organizing choices can affect and mold culture, it is difficult to establish culture directly. Leaders cannot implement a new "shared belief" simply by announcing it. They can, however, cultivate a desired belief or value by modeling behaviors consistent with that belief, by basing new priorities and programs on that belief, by telling stories that showcase that belief, and by aligning organizing choices to drive the desired culture. But leaders' influence on the final side of the cube will always be less straightforward than on the other types of organizing choices. And of course, if leadership behaviors are out of line with cultural elements required by new strategic aspirations, those aspirations will be difficult to attain.

Like Jeff Bezos, many leaders do realize how much their own language and behavior affects their organization's culture. That's why it's worth thinking through this side of the cube: considering what sort of culture is required for the new strategy and explicitly calling out the leaders' responsibilities for generating those new behaviors through new choices based on important values.

Radical Alignment and Trade-offs

We've talked through all six sides of the cube. We've said that it's crucial that all of these systems are doing their part in delivering strategy.

Now let's consider another analogy to gain a deeper understanding of how a set of systems ideally work in alignment. The pronghorn antelope of the North American plains has been dubbed "the world's premier ultrarunning animal, the best distance runner that muscle and bone and blood could produce."[13] These creatures are highly specialized for maximum aerobic capacity. The biologist Bernd Heinrich compares them to another mammal of similar build—the goat, which has excellent climbing ability rather than running ability— to make the point that though both have the same basic physiological systems, in each animal these systems are aligned toward very different survival strategies. He writes:

> In all structural aspects . . . that relate to rate of oxygen use, the antelopes [are] superior to the goats. Antelopes have more massive windpipes, three times larger lung volumes, greater gas diffusion capacity through lung tissue, an oversized heart, more cardiac output, greater amounts of hemoglobin concentration in the blood, more muscle mass, and greater numbers of mitochondria and hence more oxidative enzymes in their muscles. . . . In short, the antelopes' superb running capacity relative to the goats' does not depend on any novel mechanism. There is no magic. Instead, the antelopes' unique capacity is achieved by enhancing a specific suite of many of their normal mammalian features. There are no tricks. No one adaptation by itself makes the difference. Pronghorns are just better at everything that affects sustained running speed.[14]

Likewise, the systems in a winning organization must be better than its competitors at everything that affects its chosen point of differentiation. Tinkering in only one area is not enough. The radical alignment that is called for involves compromises as well. Antelopes, for example, store little energy in the form of body fat and have very small stomachs, adaptations that presumably conserve body weight. Consequently, they must refuel frequently on high-energy food.[15] But these compromises work for the pronghorns because they enable the animals to achieve an extraordinary ability to run and thus escape predators. Organization alignment also means living with trade-offs. Executives who don't make trade-offs end up with a "prongoat" that neither runs faster nor climbs better than competitors.

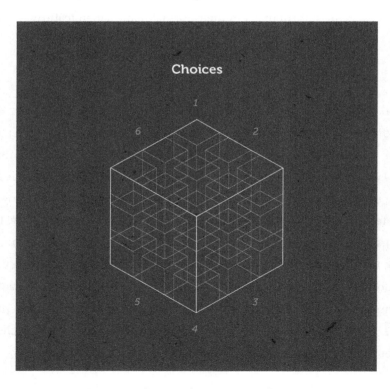

Figure 1.5: Elements of Organization Alignment

Achieving Alignment

Earlier, we stressed that leaders need to recognize that one of their chief duties is that of alignment leader. An alignment leader's approach to organizational change helps ensure that all the systems of the organization are designed and resourced in concert so they deliver marketplace differentiation.

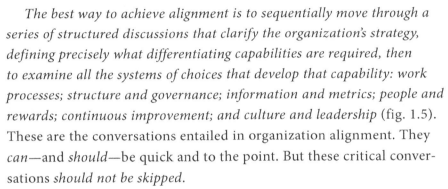

> *Above all, alignment leaders are alignment-minded.*
> *They know that true differentiation is by design.*

The best way to achieve alignment is to sequentially move through a series of structured discussions that clarify the organization's strategy, defining precisely what differentiating capabilities are required, then to examine all the systems of choices that develop that capability: work processes; structure and governance; information and metrics; people and rewards; continuous improvement; and culture and leadership (fig. 1.5). These are the conversations entailed in organization alignment. They *can*—and *should*—be quick and to the point. But these critical conversations *should not be skipped*.

A good example of a leader who learned the importance of such systematic organization alignment efforts is Ernest Jimenez, whose story opened this chapter. Jimenez's human resources partner was Jonathon Jones. Jones had been with the company long enough to be well-versed in its lengthy history of acquisitions and periodic reorganizations and spin-offs. For many years, organization design at this company had too often meant moving around the boxes—boxology.

But in the months prior to Jimenez's new assignment, some areas of the company had begun to approach restructuring in a new way. Leaders were first engaging in a series of conversations to clarify strategy and then to carefully identify what work in the organization had the most strategic impact. These discussions informed changes to the boxes and reporting lines in their organizational charts and were followed by even more work to align other organizing choices to the new strategy and structure.

The leaders had been consistently following a *sequence* for approaching organization design decisions, and they had also explored the many *types of organizing choices* beyond structure that can affect whether or not a strategy is realized.

Jones had been a part of this new approach to organization design, and he urged a very willing Jimenez to try his hand at these more systemic realignment tactics.

So Jimenez joined in-country leaders to review the value they wished to offer through the new commercial business and the distinctive work that would be necessary to drive that value, and then to design the new commercial business. What the group recognized is that as a multi-strategy business, the team had to be split into two divisions. Previously, the new commercial jobs had reported up through the same lines as the residential business. Now the leaders created a separate group for the commercial business. In other words, they used structure to enable their desired outcome. By breaking the commercial sales jobs off from the residential division, the leadership team enabled a greater focus on the new commercial business.

But they went far beyond structure and established new commercial sales processes, decision rights for the new commercial group, measures to gauge their success, jobs that would be staffed with the competencies required by the new business, and reward programs aligned to the commercial market.

As Jimenez learned, the best and most impactful organizational designs align a robust set of organizing choices to deliver the organization's strategy—not just the boxes on the organization chart. Organization aligners think through their strategy and translate it into organization reality.

Summary: Leading Optimal System Alignment

Leaders who are results-oriented are also savvy about organization alignment. They assemble and calibrate robust systems of organizing choices that work together toward the desired end. It is not just about moving around boxes. Rather, it is an extended, thoughtful adaptation of each system of the organizational antelope to become the most well-adapted creature in your marketplace ecology.

Boxology is junk-food science—an appealing practice because it is cheap, well-marketed, and satiating—but it usually doesn't contribute to long-term organization health and may even diminish it. Organization alignment, on the other hand, is whole-food science. Healthy eating takes more planning and discipline up front but results in more vitality and a greater ability to execute what is really important to you. Organizations that want to do better will slow down long enough to answer the right questions in the proper sequence covering all the relevant systems that may be holding them back from peak performance.

Key Organization Alignment Concepts

Each chapter in this book will end with a list of keys or principles for successful organization alignment. Following are the twelve key points that we covered in this chapter:

- Articulate the strategy, including trade-offs: state what unique value *will* be offered and what value *will not* be offered.

- Lay out the strategic capabilities required by the organization to successfully implement the strategy and its accompanying trade-offs.

- Imagine new and unique ways of doing work in the organization that will deliver differentiation in the marketplace.

- Group work and people into divisions, teams, departments, and jobs that clearly define their impact on the strategy and the creation or enhancement of differentiating capabilities.

- Redesign existing business processes, because if the work in an organization does not change, not much will change in marketplace results.

- Clarify decision rights to accomplish what needs to be accomplished with the least confusion about who is responsible for what.

- Design metrics to drive the desired outcomes and behaviors.

- Prioritize technology investments with a clear sense of the strategic impact.

- Revamp people selection processes, employee development practices, performance management systems, and reward systems if necessary to align with the ultimate aims.

- Consider habits regarding organization learning, ensuring that you continually review and improve performance.

- Identify cultural elements such as values and norms that are strategically important. Scrutinize leadership behaviors to ensure they reinforce espoused cultural beliefs.

- Use an organization alignment model to help you consider the full range of organizing choices, including work processes, structure, and other management systems. Remember that structure is just one aspect of a successful organization architecture.

What You Can Do Now

Jimenez and Jones are good examples of an executive and a change partner working together to get the alignment work done and to support the resulting changes.

Now think about the organizational challenge you selected at the end of the introduction. Consider the following questions based on the stumbling and building blocks discussed in this chapter. Then identify your next steps to move forward in solving the challenge.

	Alignment leader responses	Change partner responses
What is clear or not clear about how an organizational change will deliver unique customer value or capabilities?		
What information/data do I need to validate whether a structural change is needed?		
What misalignments do I see in the work, structure/ governance, information/ metrics, people/rewards, continuous improvement, and leadership/culture systems of our organization?		
How could I devise an approach to address the organizational challenges we are facing using a process that considers all organization systems, not just structure?		

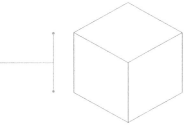

CHAPTER 2

HOW TO DESIGN
THE RIGHT ORGANIZATION

In the last chapter, we explained how the most effective organization alignment initiatives move through a series of structured conversations in order to get the organization systems positioned to create the differentiating capabilities required by the strategy. We said this effort requires that leaders engage in some up-front planning and put forth additional effort above and beyond tinkering with the boxes on the organizational chart or launching a Lean Six Sigma project.

But what if you are not quite sure what topics your leadership team needs to discuss to prepare for realignment? What if you do not have the time for these conversations (even though we said it can and should be quick)? What should you do if you just do not have the mental energy to focus on this stuff, because your team is so busy running the business?

You might be inclined to call in a consulting firm to tackle this work for you.

OFF-THE-SHELF ORGANIZATIONS
STUMBLING BLOCK 2

Robert Underwood did just that—he called in a consulting firm to help his team when they faced a big organization alignment challenge. Underwood was the CEO of an insurance provider that confronted a fundamental dilemma about the corporate ownership structure—a question that many insurance companies struggle with at one point or another. Should they remain a mutual insurance company, owned by policyholders, or should they sell stock?

Underwood and his team commissioned an in-depth study to ferret out the pros and the cons of this proposition and decided, in the end, not to go public. "There were great benefits of remaining a mutual insurer," he says, "but it was obvious that we were not taking advantage of some of those benefits." The leadership team therefore decided to pursue a new strategy with a laser focus on gaining customer trust and delivering industry-leading customer service.

They recognized that the organization did not currently support many of the new activities they would need to accomplish the company's new mission. They believed a new structure was required and other organizing choices as well. But Underwood wasn't sure how to regroup people in order to best deliver the new, differentiating work activities he had in mind. So he invited a major global consulting firm to provide advice.

The executive team spent half a day with the consultants reviewing several exemplary organizational structures, from both the insurance industry and other outstanding enterprises. They weighed the pros and cons of various formations. Then the consultants turned to Underwood's team and asked them to choose the "right one" for their company.

Underwood found himself at a crossroads. Despite this expert survey of the most effective structures in the industry and beyond, he felt grave misgivings. He was leery of adopting something based on the strategies of other organizations. He felt the options embodied other cultures, not his company's. *He had just encountered Stumbling Block 2: off-the shelf organizations.*

Underwood was not alone in his misgivings—other members of the executive team felt restricted and obstructed by the simple multiple-choice question the consultants posed. It seemed to the team that something as fundamental and strategic as how the business was aligned could not be answered in the same way that one might darken a bubble on a test form.

Underwood realized that an organizational structure should not be selected from a restricted set of options. It should be tailor-made to fit the unique needs of a company or institution. What's more, alignment is as much about the process of discussing options, weighing benefits and risks, and reaching an agreement as a leadership team on how best to design the organization to achieve marketplace distinction as it is about the resulting choices. Leaders need to dialogue together to generate creative momentum and climb the path that heads toward new ways of thinking. Hearing a presentation or reading a report and then holding a short discussion will never *be* an adequate approach for making a decision about something as momentous as the alignment of strategy, capabilities, and choices, and it will never *feel* adequate, either.

TAILOR TO STRATEGY
BUILDING BLOCK 2

Search as you may, there is no optimal set of structures "out there" that you can discover and from which you can select the ideal template to base your organization design on. While consultants or your own research may certainly uncover some basic organizing options and even best practices about how to group people and teams according to functions, products, geographies, or customers, for example, adopting these forms will not create the change you desire—unless you also think through how they might help you achieve the intentions of your strategy and your business model. Within a single industry, organizations may craft many varied organizational structures. In fact, doing so helps them differentiate themselves from each other in the marketplace. *The practice of tailoring a structure to fit your organization's unique strategy is Building Block 2.*

Strategic Trade-offs and Organization Alignment

What is best for you and your organization will be unique because of the strategy that your team, and only your team, has chosen to pursue. As we mentioned in the last chapter, a critical but oft overlooked component of strategy is to identify a clear set of *strategic trade-offs.* Because resources are always limited, to create an organization alignment that fits your needs, you must know your strategic trade-offs so that you can ensure they are cascaded throughout the organization.

A good example of a company that knows its trade-offs is Starbucks, which we also mentioned in the last chapter. Starbucks' strategy is to offer a product/experience bundle of high-quality, innovative coffee drinks; personalized service; and an upscale environment with a relaxed ambience (and fast wireless!). But saying what they *will do* is only half of the story. They are also very clear on what they *will not do*—their trade-offs. For one thing, their prices are higher. For another, access is generally less convenient than the drive-through at McDonalds or Dunkin Donuts or Tim Horton's. The lines inside are often longer as well.

As we saw, Starbucks' organization design is aligned to its strategy and trade-offs. For example, to make all the variations of coffee drinks offered, Starbucks baristas undergo extensive training. After making such an investment in education and development, the company wants to ensure these employees stay around a while, so they offer their massive part-time workforce (about 100,000) full benefits. This is expensive—a trade-off—but it results in turnover that is less than a quarter of the industry average.[1] Extensive training and benefits for the part-time workforce are organizing choices made by Starbucks that flow from their strategy. They are well-known as a company that "puts people over profits." Commensurate with these values and choices is the fact that the human resources organization at Starbucks ("partner resources") reports directly to the CEO.[2] A cookie-cutter organization design for a food retailer might never include these important considerations, but they are essential to Starbucks' distinctiveness.

Then there is Apple. Steve Jobs was obsessed with great design based on an aesthetic of intense simplicity. He knew that consumers would want products that were beautifully designed and thinner and smaller than what the competition offered. But attending to the details of a few great products meant rejecting the temptation to tackle many more products or expand into many new markets. "It's only by saying no that you can concentrate on the things that are really important," he said.[3] Apple's organization design reflects this philosophy as well. There are no product ownership roles at the highest level—only functional groups such as design, engineering, operations, and marketing. Instead, collaboration is fostered through frequent product reviews built into the development process.[4]

Can your leadership team identify your trade-offs? It is often easy to see trade-offs in other companies, but can you articulate your own? There are no optical drives in any Apple Airs or data ports in iPads. Has your enterprise similarly been able to say no to your equivalent of optical drives and data ports? Apple may lose some customers who want an integrated DVD player. They are okay with that. Starbucks may lose some customers on a tight budget who are in a big hurry. They are okay with that.

Saying yes to a customer you should have said no to means saying no to a customer you should have said yes to.

Do you know when to say no? Do the people throughout your company? One of the greatest ways to empower employees is to gift them with strong strategic nos. An example from a company that produces and sells high-quality pet food shows how one plant leader ensures that his employees understand those nos. A team member working late at night in bulk receiving was presented with a truckload of sub-quality corn—a key ingredient in dry dog food. This employee was well-informed of quality tolerances and knew that the corn was subpar, and he also knew that he had the authority to reject the load. But still he hesitated. While the driver waited, he took a tray of the corn up to the front office, covered in corn dust with his face mask pushed down around his neck. He found the plant manager and told him about the problem.

"Do you believe the corn is sub-standard?" the plant manager asked.

"Yes," replied the team member. "It's been tested and it contains too much moisture."

"Then what should you do?" replied the plant manager.

"This corn should be rejected, but we may run out of raw ingredients and have to shut down production."

"What should you do?" repeated the plant manager.

"We should reject the load," replied the team member, "but I need someone to authorize that."

"You already have the authority for that—it's part of your job," said the plant manager.

"Then I'll have to reject the corn," said the team member, and headed back out to the receiving area.

The plant manager reinforced an important strategic no in the mind of this team member by insisting that he exercise his own decision-making power to do what was right, even at the risk of shutting down the dry product line. Factory utilization is vitally important to keep costs down for this company, but it takes a strategic backseat to high-quality product.

There are a myriad of ways an organization can compete; a myriad of nos that can be spoken for every yes. Organizations compete by assembling a few yeses and many, many nos together in their own signature way. These trade-offs guide organization alignment at the operational level. Saying yes to some strategic pursuits means saying yes to the organization processes, structures, technologies, and jobs that will support those pursuits by showering them with resources. Saying no to other pursuits means eliminating work activities, software, departments, and incompatible measures and reward systems that are likewise extraneous.

The trade-offs selected by your strategic team must be clear and explicit. They must be cascaded to every person in the company to guide the yes-no decisions made daily in work routines and at customer touch points. Anyone who chooses tasks, spends money, or speaks to a customer should know the big yeses and the big nos. These polarizing points guide supervisors assigning work priorities, customer service associates on the phone, and salespeople facing potential clients. *If strategic trade-offs aren't made by the lead organization aligners, then they will be made by someone else, somewhere in the organization based on expediency, individual preference, politics, customer pressure, or individual performance measures—not based on strategy or alignment.*

Strategy can never be fully implemented until the strategic trade-offs show up at the activity level in the organization. But off-the-shelf templates of organization charts do not identify the implicit trade-offs. They do not depict the yeses and the nos. The only way to define those is in thorough alignment deliberations about strategy and capability.

Robert Underwood was wary of the off-the-shelf organizational charts the high-priced consultants had lined up for him. So he met with his leadership team privately and after spending a little time exploring alternative approaches to finding a new structure, they selected a different methodology for developing their changing organization. They chose to go a bit slower and work through a series of discussions about their marketplace, their own unique strategy, their differentiating capabilities, their trade-offs, and the implications for the way they grouped the organization into divisions and teams. They chose to involve more people in the effort. And they decided to look beyond structure and think about other changes that would bring about a new day.

"I liked the idea that we would fashion our structure from our mission and vision, not someone else's," says Underwood. "I also liked the idea that we were not going to take someone else's structure and try to force our company into it—that we would build this up from within with our own talent and our own vision of what the future was."

Developing a Signature Organization Alignment

Limiting your organization structure to the options presented on any predetermined list will, at best, produce unsatisfactory results. Your strategy is unique, and therefore your organization capabilities must be unique. It is your job to assemble a distinctive array of organizing choices configured for your specific strategy, including trade-offs. Developing these capabilities will not only enable you to win but will also shut out others from duplicating your success, as tightly orchestrated organization systems are resistant to competitive copycatting.

Yet it is extremely tempting to copycat what you see working for others. As you get started, you may consider benchmarking the most successful organizations in your industry and trying to replicate their success. It is important to remember that since all organizing options include downsides or trade-offs, choosing someone else's structure also means adopting their trade-offs. Then you would have a copied design, not a distinctive design, with trade-offs that may not suit your organization at all. Even if it were possible to adopt the full set of design choices that has been successful for another company—which it is not—doing so would by definition make it impossible to create any distinctiveness of your own.

Remember that structure does not build organization capability. Work activities and other organizing choices do. Structure only enables people to work more strategically—on the right tasks with the right people. If you really wanted to copy another company, you would have to duplicate all their organizing choices. But again, this does not work very well. Take Southwest Airlines, for example. It is one of the most persistently successful airlines in the world: of the forty plus airlines that have tried to mimic Southwest's original no-frills, highly efficient business model, none have survived as strong direct competitors. That is because Southwest's activities are embedded in a web of other organizing choices that create their signature culture and business model. Indeed, it is nearly impossible to copy all the organizing choices of another company.

Again, this means that your team will need to align the organizing choices that are uniquely suited to your strategy. You do this by considering many different choices, weighing their fit and advantages and disadvantages, and finally selecting the set that best reflects the strategic trade-offs you are willing to live with.

Strategic Tailoring Using Linkages

Stumbling Blocks 1 and 2 have addressed common mistakes regarding organization structure. Building Block 1 warns leaders not to place all their hopes in revamping their organizational chart but instead to align all systems to strategy. Building Block 2 cautions against adopting ready-made structures rather than developing a highly customized organization design. A final word about structural change before moving on: Structural problems can appear to be the source of disconnects between disparate groups that need to work together. But resolving such problems may not require a full-fledged redesign of the organizational chart; often, a simple retooling of linkages may be enough.

Linkages are mechanisms that bring together people who need to work across boundaries. They help to create shared experience, shared mentality, and shared interest in people from different groups who need to be networked. Because they connect people who aren't otherwise in contact with one another through the reporting structure but who nevertheless could benefit by sharing their ideas about how to please customers and work efficiently, linkages mitigate the downsides inherent in the formal organization structure. Linkages allow the structure to win because they minimize structural trade-offs.

Linkages can exist in a myriad of forms. They may include practices or artifacts as simple as rules and policies, shared goals, open forums, and training, to more complicated devices such as process management teams, communities of practices, and matrix organizations.

Linkages need not be formal—naturally occurring informal conversations or shared values throughout the organization may be enough to connect people from different groups. The very strongest linkage develops when a leader with a collaborative mind-set spontaneously recognizes the connections between his or her group and the rest of the organization and acts to bring people together to tighten these bonds.

In many ways the organization's cultural values determine how much linking happens naturally and informally. An enterprise with a network of leaders who habitually reach out to each other to coordinate and collaborate may not need many formal linking mechanisms.

Even so, a few formal efforts to help people align on an important process or strategic priority can close existing gaps or ensure that a new structure does not break apart crucial ongoing interactions that may be practically invisible prior to a big change in the organizational chart. For example, a new master data management group created *business rules* to link all the people entering product data in different groups throughout the company. A fledgling shared IT group created a project prioritization *forum* to ensure business leaders worked together to determine the best way to utilize limited IT resources. A new sales group at an agriculture products business that formed when two product lines were integrated created *shared metrics* to generate enthusiasm for selling bundled products. These are each examples of linkages chosen for their strength at mitigating the risks associated with a new structure.

We can see another example of the power of linkages in a medical devices company undergoing rapid growth. During this period, one division of the company found it was taking longer and longer to get products to market. So they geared up for structure change, assuming that their burgeoning size necessitated an org chart adjustment. As the organization was getting larger, cross-boundary collaboration was falling apart. But upon closer examination, it was clear that the downsides of their current design were actually quite workable and that bolstering new methods of helping people interact would likely be enough to speed up the development and production timeline. Among other efforts, they added a vetting process to evaluate new projects, and they reinforced an existing PMO (project management office) with new processes and additional talent.

Recognizing the hazards inherent in any organization structure and allaying them with linkages can be as powerful and impactful as actually reshuffling the organizational chart—and often a lot less painful.

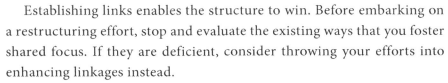

Linkages trump structure.

Establishing links enables the structure to win. Before embarking on a restructuring effort, stop and evaluate the existing ways that you foster shared focus. If they are deficient, consider throwing your efforts into enhancing linkages instead.

In fact, if your organization has never appropriately mitigated the downsides of your current structure with a few formal linkages, you really do not know how effective the existing structure could be. In our experience, organizations that do not mitigate their structures spin their organization design (and their people) every twelve to eighteen months. Though no structure will suffice forever, this cycle is much shorter than it generally needs to be.

Simple fact: if you have put together a new organizational chart, you are not done with your new design until you have recognized the vulnerabilities of your creation and found ways to shore them up. Be sure you take time to acknowledge the risks in any structure—current or proposed—and make a plan to diminish those downsides. Someone else's organization structure or a best practice organization model cannot do this for you. Off-the-shelf organizations don't come with warning labels. Your team alone must do this kind of mitigation work.

Summary: Eschewing the Multiple-Choice Design

When it's time to revise your organizational structure, resist the impulse to call in an expert to lay out a set of options for you. Instead, engage your change partner and gather the right group of leaders to systematically discuss your strategy, the capabilities your organization needs, and possible ways to align the systems that have grown up through the years on the other side of your conference room door.

Without a doubt, these are difficult, high-stakes discussions, and certainly your team can benefit from the help of an interlocutor to guide you through the process. It may make sense to turn to a skilled and engaged change partner within your organization for help, such as a colleague in human resources, organization effectiveness, organization design, strategy, information systems, or continuous improvement (Lean Six Sigma). She can prepare questions or exercises to move your team toward your targeted outcomes, to challenge your assumptions, to nudge you when you are stuck, and to generally keep you on topic.

A consultant can help in this way, too. But before you select one, consider the difference between an expert consultant and a process-driven consultant. An *expert* consultant offers answers to your questions; a *process-driven* consultant provides a crafted sequence of questions to help you reach your answers. For instance, an expert consultant might offer a multiple-choice selection of organization structures and ask you to pick one to implement, while a process consultant will provide a path for making a decision about a new structure or set of design choices, but she will let the most appropriate options emerge in the course of your team's discussions.

In the next chapter, we will explore the vital importance of interactive conversations in generating and spreading insight about organization alignment. For now, we offer some specific questions that can guide the dialogue:

- How will we win in the marketplace?

- What trade-offs will we make?

- What capabilities will differentiate us from the competition?

- Of all the work we could possibly do, what is of greatest strategic importance to us? What work can be done at par? What work can we eliminate?

- What rationale should guide us in configuring our resources to deliver our strategic core?

- How will people work together across boundaries?

Answering these questions will help you further define your strategy, your structure, and the linking mechanisms that limit the liabilities of your structure. They will help you make difficult decisions that consultants and other experts cannot make for you, decisions that must be made by you and your team as the leaders—the chief aligners—of your organization. Making these decisions marks the beginnings of true organizational alignment.

Key Organization Alignment Concepts

Now we can add four more concepts to our ongoing list of keys to successful organization alignment:

- Develop a tailored organizing option that fits your strategy and the trade-offs you are willing to make.
- Identify the downsides of the organizing option you have chosen.
- Don't copy competitors.
- Think through ways of linking people whose work is interdependent across boundaries to avoid or mitigate the downsides inherent in your structure.

What You Can Do Now

If you are ready to gather your leadership team, your organization change partner can help. She can help you decide if you really do need structure change, or if bolstering your linking mechanisms or other organizing choices will do the trick. She will help you devise a plan for cascading trade-off decisions throughout the organization.

Now go back to the organization challenge you identified at the end of the introduction and continued writing about at the end of the last chapter. Consider the following questions based on the stumbling and building blocks presented in this chapter.

	Alignment leader responses	Change partner responses
What strategic trade-offs should we consider making in our organization so we can align our resources and choices to the most important work?		
Where is our organization structure misaligned to our intended strategy?		
What are the prevailing assumptions in our industry about how to structure our organization and deploy our resources to go to market? Are there industry benchmarks that seem to predominate our thinking?		
How do these prevailing assumptions spark strategic insight or constrain the strategic options you are considering?		
How might we overcome the boundaries set up in the organization structure through proper linkages?		

CHAPTER 3

WHO TO INVOLVE IN THE ALIGNMENT PROCESS

This chapter begins with the dangers of the *closet organization redesign*.

A closet organization redesign is when a leader selects a few members of his team and sequesters himself with them to develop a new organization design without informing or warning anyone else.

The widespread use of this approach leads us to conclude that many leaders believe it is best to limit design work to just a few trusted colleagues.

◆ THE SECRET SOCIETY
STUMBLING BLOCK 3

The leaders at a pharmaceutical division of a multinational conglomerate were big believers in this practice. The division's vice president wanted sales, which for years had been organized into strong products groups with jobs that were rewarded for deep product expertise, to become more customer intimate. So she brought a very limited group of her leaders together to reorganize sales into customer-focused groups.

Then they announced the change and launched the new rearranged configuration almost immediately.

The new sales teams started up in alarming disarray. Though the leaders explained the strategic reasoning for the changes, the employees simply did not know enough about the intent of the new design to work effectively in a new way. The head of sales had not been part of the team who made the decisions and so found the product-focused worldview that had shaped his career and driven his leadership accomplishments abandoned literally overnight. He floundered.

Likewise, product specialists sitting in their new cross-product teams were at a loss, tasked now to sell complete solutions, or groups of bundled products. Their training and trail of work experience had been geared toward one type of product. How could they sell six other offerings at the same time—never mind the challenge of setting prices in a strategic yet harmonized way? How does a person go about interacting with team members and relating to clients to sell a solution? Because the specialists had not been part of imagining this new world, they had not fully grasped it, and thus could not execute it. They knew only in concept what they were supposed to do; they had even less intuition about what former ways of working now needed to be cast aside. The trade-offs of the new strategy had not been articulated, so the team couldn't fathom giving up the tried-and-true sales practices they had relied on for years.

Since so many change efforts proceed in this manner, it is no wonder that a majority of them fail. Assuming that people *will want* to change and *will be able* to change if only the new direction is laid out for them by their leaders is a common and unfortunate misperception. *Stumbling Block 3 is the practice of restricting major organization change decisions and planning to a very limited group of leaders.*

What advantages do leaders see in restricting involvement to a secret society and keeping a restructure under wraps?

One worry is that when people throughout an organization know that a change is imminent, they will get nervous for their jobs. Change is scary, especially if it involves the word "restructure." Even when people are assured that their livelihoods are not at risk, they fret about whom they will be reporting to, whom they will be working with, and how their work will be different. In an earnest display of empathy or an attempt to minimize the business impact, leaders sometimes try to protect workers from angst.

A second reason why leaders limit the number of people involved in the change process is to keep the lid on any unpleasant goals related to the project. It is difficult to lay all your cards on the table and announce that a 15 percent expense reduction is in the works. It is safer to reveal that news only to a group of top leaders, or even to hire consultants to help accomplish such difficult deliverables.

A third reason to constrain the number of participants in organization design is the assumption that most people will not be able to think beyond their own interests and work for the good of the organization. The thought is that their input will favor something that works well for themselves personally or for their current group or project priorities, but at the expense of long-term strategic interests.

But protecting employees from worry, keeping reduction targets quiet, or underestimating people's organizational altruism are tactics that come at a cost. The missed opportunity is the revolution in thinking that occurs through participation in a realignment process. A leader's or contributor's ability to execute a new design is not just about knowing its rationale. It is also about being so steeped in imagining the new way of being that he or she knows what it is *not* as well as what it *is*. People who participate in design decisions see a bigger picture because they know what has been left on the cutting-room floor. They know what to do and what not to do anymore. They can anticipate roadblocks and improvise ways around them because they grasp the full intent of the change.

At the pharmaceutical division, for example, teams had trouble selecting loss leaders for their new solution offerings in order to gain their customers' attention. Their old way of getting rewarded for product margin stymied them in the new world. But if these sales representatives had been involved in the organization design discussions, they would have been more informed and thus more nimble at improvising new reward methods to accommodate new sales approaches.

Clearly leaders at the pharmaceutical division initially missed the substantial benefits they would have reaped by having broader participation in the alignment process. The first and most obvious upside would have been a better design. The wisdom of a team with a diversity of experience exceeds the wisdom of a few leaders. If even a handful of members of this sales force had been a part of the discussion, they would have alerted the leaders to some of the risks inherent in the move to a customer focus, such as misaligned training and reward practices.

But the second benefit of high involvement is the change management benefit. When leaders select one set of organizing choices over another, they do so because they believe that the new set of choices will deliver better results. They make cause-and-effect assumptions: "If we group people a certain way, allocate decision rights in a certain way, train people in a certain way, then they will act in a certain way that will help our company." They also come to agreements, often implicit, about what is no longer as important as it once was. It is folly to think people will implement the design as anticipated if they do not share the same assumptions.

 *You cannot achieve different results without helping people learn how to think differently.*

Whether or not leaders have participated in the process, they will have to absorb and commit to the trade-offs associated with the choices that have been made. What better way for leaders to internalize the trade-offs than for them to be part of the alignment effort that vets those decisions.

CO-CREATE
BUILDING BLOCK 3

Building Block 3 is the practice of involving a broad group of leaders and subject matter experts in organization alignment both to gain the benefits of their thinking and to enfold them in the thinking revolution inherent in the process.

The core development that makes new organization alignments successful is a change in organizational thinking that results in behavior change. In this book, we have advocated using a series of structured discussions to clarify strategy and craft an organization that can produce the desired effects of that strategy. To help organizations walk through these discussions, we often suggest that they produce a collection of charts, diagrams, and other graphics along the way that codify the outcomes of their discussions. But the new alignment is not embodied in these artifacts. Rather, it is embodied in the minds of participants as they jointly arrive at new beliefs about what will produce important capabilities in their organization. Thinking coalesces through the experience of asking and answering crucial questions together, of co-creating the organizational design. No presentation deck, worksheet, or organization chart can ever replace the shared experience of together articulating ideas, concerns, and insights.

The Interactive Alignment Approach

Indeed, for optimal results, organization alignment *must* be an interactive process where participants come to mutual insight through conversation, joint decision making, and the evaluation of trade-offs. Making strategic decisions is like setting off on an adventure with uncertain outcomes. Leaders hope that the journey will culminate in triumph but understand it will likely be fraught with perils and setbacks. Anxiety marks these uneasy strategic decisions: leaders feel both anticipation and dread when they see the possibility of changing the trajectory of the organization. As we said before, *developing new capabilities takes time, and backing off from old capabilities takes courage.* When alignment teams talk and together grapple with what is best for their institutions, they gain confidence—and often feel exuberant—in the resulting shared point of view. They begin implicitly to harmonize their individual plans of action. These are the ideal conditions for the unrestrained, coordinated action that characterizes successful change. Conversation is so important for this kind of social achievement that philosophers have called it "communicative action."[1]

The experience of reaching shared insights in a good interactive alignment session can be surprising. For example, during two days of intense conversations at a global supplier in the food industry, the executive team together made some significant decisions that shifted the balance of organization power. One of the participants later approached the facilitator, smiling, and with a twinkle in his eye said, "You scoundrel." Then he said it again, with emphasis: "You *scoundrel*! I would have never thought a group of executives would do this to themselves. Congratulations. I can see the path they took that led them to do it."

The more people are involved in alignment deliberations, the more likely the effort will result in substantial organizational and behavioral change, and thus improvements to the bottom line. Organization alignment discussions are where change management begins, not several days or weeks later when a beautifully packaged presentation is pitched to the enterprise. It is best to broaden alignment participation as much as you can, and then work to replicate the experience for other enterprise members in a cascade down through the organization.

While we heartily recommend taking an interactive approach to organization alignment, it's important to recognize from the get-go that a more participative process will take more time and require more coordination and planning. There are other downsides:

- Involving lots of people early in the alignment process will elongate the period of uncertainty.

- Leaders will need to boldly articulate the essentials of the alignment, even if that means budget cuts or workforce reduction.

- Leaders will need to trust alignment participants to put the interests of the enterprise before their own parochial concerns.

- Leaders will need to communicate expected behaviors and champion enterprise thinking.

What helps assuage the risks inherent in high involvement is a clean organization alignment process—a reliable road map from the old organization to the new, a tried-and-true method of getting the Rubik's Cube back in order. For example, if alignment participants are presented with a plan for putting one foot in front of the other, they can move from strategy to aligned organizing choices while avoiding political infighting over resources. If they are shown how to identify and mitigate the downside of any design, they can agree on which trade-offs they are willing to live with and avoid circling tirelessly, trying to find the one perfect design. If they evaluate together what work has the greatest strategic impact, they can agree on what work should be heavily resourced, and settle into working toward the greatest efficiency of all other types of work. If they can get clear about accountabilities, power struggles in the new organization will be diminished. If they together prioritize information system projects to support the new design, they can give their IT departments some clarity and peace. If they align performance measures and reward systems, they will know up front how their pay and incentives will be affected.

Consider a rental car company that was hurting significantly after the 2008 downturn in the global marketplace. On a beautiful winter Monday, crisp and cold, one of the regional presidents, Juliet Chevalier, brought her ten-person executive team into a conference room. "We have to reduce costs throughout the organization," she said, "including my staff. At the end of this week, there needs to be two or three fewer positions in this room reporting to me. The rest of the reduction will occur in middle management." She essentially asked her team to determine which of their own positions should be eliminated while at the same time requiring them to look out for the good of the organization.

So those executives went to work. They clarified their strategy. They articulated their trade-offs. They determined what kind of organization was needed to support their future capabilities. On Friday, the ten reported out their work to Chevalier, identifying only eight reports in the new structure. They had designed away two of their own jobs.

Here is what we love: they thanked Chevalier. Previously in their careers, they said, external firms had always been called in to decide how cuts and restructures would play out across the enterprise. But these leaders had composed the new design themselves. "We know there's at least two of us in the room who won't have jobs on this leadership team," they said, "but we understand the organization that we are going to be implementing. We put it together. We understand the trade-offs. We would rather do it ourselves than have some external firm do it to us."

What this example shows is that the people who work in an organization can reliably and expertly redesign it, even if it involves workforce cuts. Even if they design themselves out of a job. We constantly work with teams who reallocate or eliminate their own jobs, professionally and amicably. A group at a big box retailer, for example, began with a modest cost-cutting goal and realized at some point in the alignment that the conclusions they were reaching eliminated a small but long-standing and respected group of expert technician-managers. One of those managers sat on the alignment team. Their final days together became poignant as the team realized they would soon be bidding farewell to this admired manager. But work carried on apace. One team member found the entire experience career altering. Though he lamented the loss of the team member, he said he wished everyone could be part of an organization alignment team. He relished experiencing the mind-set shift that occurred as he learned to think from a holistic, strategic perspective.

The Organization Alignment Team

What criteria should you use to select people for the team? Aside from assembling a group with a wide range of expertise, here are a few qualities to look for:

1. People who can focus on a new direction and strategy as the top priority

2. Team players who do not view their job or department's success as good enough

3. People effective at communicating and debating ideas, but who can give themselves over to consensus after healthy deliberation

4. People mature enough to fully participate even knowing that their role and others around them may be impacted

5. Individuals with high learning agility

6. People who can take a broad enterprise perspective

In selecting these folks, keep these considerations in mind:

- Look for natural change agents and early adopters who are strong influencers. If others in the organization tend to follow them naturally, they can be powerful catalysts for change.

- Consider high-potential individuals and use this as a development opportunity.

- Identify key leaders who will most likely resist the change (skeptics and traditionalists), but include them only if their resistance would create significant barriers to successful implementation. You will need their support and buy-in to implement the plan.

Cross-functional teams of top- and mid-level leaders are often extraordinary organization aligners. The experience is an invaluable growth opportunity.

To be dubbed organization aligners for a few weeks converts people into alignment leaders for the rest of their careers.

Indeed, strategic capability for organization alignment is built when people of all levels participate in alignment efforts. These are the conditions under which an entire organization becomes alignment-minded: when several layers of vice presidents, directors, and even managers and individual contributors are invited to make organization alignment decisions, communicate those decisions to their peers, and be a part of leading the implementation of what they have had a hand in designing.

	NOW	LATER
The Secret Society *(Easier Now)*	Easier (faster) to make alignment decisions Involves fewer people Minimizes disruption to everyday work Costs less now	Harder for people to adapt to change Slower to implement Higher risk of misaligned organization Doesn't build change capability Mid-level leaders don't experience alignment deliberations Shelf life of organization change is shorter Costs more
Co-creation *(Easier Later)*	Harder (slower) to make alignment decisions Involves more people Greater disruption to everyday work if not managed well Costs more now	Easier for people to adapt to change Faster to implement Organization is more aligned Builds long-term change capability Mid-level leaders get hands-on experience with alignment Shelf life of organization change is longer Costs less

Figure 3.1: Engagement Approaches and Their Consequences

Pay Now or Pay Later

Widespread organization involvement has another advantage: though it takes more coordination and planning up front, it takes less time to execute the design. The result of high participation is widespread mutual understanding of what is to be accomplished. People know what they need to start doing and what they need to stop doing. They are less resistant because they have already imagined themselves in the new world and had time to adjust. In fact, they are often eager to get the show on the road.

Achieving high-involvement alignment costs more up front in time, money, and emotional energy. But implementation is likely to be faster and more successful. Indeed, it is pay now or pay later.

Summary: Co-creating an Aligned Organization

When you make the strategic decision to engage people from your entire workforce in organization alignment, the result will be more complete and its implementation will be faster. What's more, you'll have developed a network of holistic thinkers who have learned to be alignment-minded. You'll have created a versatile set of cube-masters, if you will, who not only think beyond their own domains but know the tools for linking all of an organization's domains together. They will be architects, not bricklayers, in Watkins's words.

High involvement is just one change management technique—albeit a powerful one. It is advisable to incorporate other change management tactics into the earliest stages of the organization alignment as well. While a full discussion of change management is beyond the scope of this book, we do want to confirm that your change partner can and should ensure that all the best techniques of change management are brought to the table early in the process, including the high-involvement approach we have endorsed.

Key Organization Alignment Concepts

Our discussion in this chapter about the importance of high involvement in an alignment effort gives us three new points to add to our list of key concepts:

- Involve many people in the organization in planning and implementing the alignment to get the best thinking—and to change thinking—throughout the ranks. (Besides, it will accelerate the time to implement!)

- Use an alignment process that has a clear road map from strategy and its trade-offs through capabilities to organization choices.

- Incorporate change management practices and tools into the organizational alignment methodology from its earliest stages.

What You Can Do Now

In this chapter we discussed the benefits of involving a wide array of leaders and subject matter experts in organization alignment work. Your organization change partner can help you find the right composition for cross-functional teams to do the work that is needed. He can help you select, charter, and steer these alignment teams.

Now return to the organization challenge you have been working on and ponder the questions that follow.

	Alignment leader responses	Change partner responses
Who typically is involved in organization alignment discussions at our enterprise?		
What about how people think in our organization needs to change as we work to realign focus, resources, and organizing choices?		
Given the challenge we are currently facing, who ought to be involved?		
How will I engage the right people and position the work that needs to be done in a constructive way?		
What is the road map we will use to ensure a clear route from strategy and its trade-offs through capabilities to choices?		

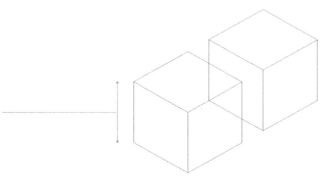

CHAPTER 4

WHEN TO SELECT THE RIGHT PEOPLE FOR NEW JOBS

A major wall coating company decided to transform from a product-focused manufacturer to a retail service provider. Their decision was based on extensive market data. Although the company still planned to produce wall coatings, they wanted to differentiate themselves in the marketplace by the experience they could offer customers at the independent retailers that sold their products.

They identified the new capabilities they would need, including new expertise in merchandising, store design, and branding, and they set about making organizing choices to drive the new strategies. They reconceived what work in their organization delivered the most strategic impact—what we call *competitive work*. They altered governance practices, and they established new metrics. All the right things. One key thing they did not do at first was to change their structure, which for over one hundred years had adhered to a functional model (with verticals such as product development, manufacturing, marketing, and sales). After some months they recognized the need to better enable the new strategy by grouping people together in different ways.

But when it came time to place talent within the new structure, they backed off from earlier commitments to assess whether their current leaders really had the competencies required by the new organization. They simply placed the old players in most of the new roles.

STARTING WITH PEOPLE
STUMBLING BLOCK 4

It's surprising how often we see this type of approach to staffing an organization that has been aligned in every other way. Staff placement ends up being just an exercise in reshuffling old friends and their familiar competencies.

Have you ever been tempted to do this? *It's Stumbling Block 4: starting with people.*

When it comes to organization alignment, it's better to start with *strategy* than with people. This is because tinkering with the arrangement of employees in an organization is not sufficient to produce organization change. We will repeat what we stated earlier: if the work of the organization does not change, then its capabilities do not change; and if capabilities do not change, then modifications to the strategy will never be realized. Likewise, if the skills and competencies of the people in the organization do not change, then the organization will not be truly aligned.

A year out from the new design, the wall coatings company had failed to gain the expected market traction. They ended up making the tough personnel changes after all. It was a waste of a year and who knows how many millions of dollars.

Staffing Over Strategy

It is a reality that preserving the jobs or the opportunities or the power of certain organizational players can be an important consideration during organization alignment. This is not necessarily inadvisable, because rewarding talent or loyalty or other merits is often good for the organization as well as for the individuals. But if decision after decision is largely based on the social consequences, then an organization may be missing the opportunity to drive the business with a marketplace motivation.

Talent by itself can't deliver strategy.

Let's look at an example. A huge global engineering firm dived into a realignment of one of its businesses. Led by a new COO, a tight team of five leaders met half days over the course of two weeks. At the end of this period, the team gathered to present their final recommendation to the company president. Before the team got far, he began flipping through the presentation deck. He found the org chart. He lingered there a few minutes, tossed it on the table, then pushed back his chair.

"Mariana," he said to the COO, "this isn't it."

The alignment team was caught off guard and slightly embarrassed. "What's wrong?" asked the COO. "Let us at least explain our rationale." The president held her off, however. "We have to have a place for Terrence, Janet, and Francois. They must have a spot in our organization, and I see them as the regional heads."

The team had not even designed a regional structure.

Despite being interviewed by the team, the company president had not been forthcoming in his expectations, truly open to the full range of alignment options, or willing to consider that the competencies of his leadership team should be evaluated against the demands of strategy. He tripped on Stumbling Block 4 and identified the people for the realigned organization before alignment leaders had determined the structure to best embody the strategy or articulated the leadership competencies required by the new jobs.

Organization Alignment as a Performance Management Mechanism

Sometimes leaders do the reverse: instead of jumping the gun on placing leaders in a realigned organization, they use organization alignment as a safe way to actually get rid of underperforming players.

Now let's look at a different division of the same engineering firm. The fifty-something executive leading it, Vishal Anantha, had thousands of engineers reporting to him from around the world; he was bright, experienced, confident. In pre-alignment interviews joined by the HR business partner, we asked Anantha to articulate the new capabilities he wanted to develop in the organization. He listed becoming more customer intimate along with other aspirations, and then he added, "I want senior leadership to get along better."

"Tell us more about that," we said.

"Well, there's a person on my team who was in contention for my job and thinks he should have gotten it. He acts out by being highly disruptive in every meeting."

So we asked, "Would this be a successful realignment if this person was still reporting to you when it's complete?" Anantha said no.

We recognized that the restructuring was primarily intended to address the issue with this individual, and we frankly shared our assessment with Anantha. We asked him if he really wanted to go through an extensive realignment to resolve these problems with a direct report. As he discussed the possibilities with us and his HR partner, he determined that what was really needed was professional coaching for this leader, not global restructuring.

To leaders who may be tempted to deal with high-profile, high-powered personality issues by camouflaging them as an alignment initiative, we say: don't do it. There are better ways to move your people in and out of position.

STAFFING FOLLOWS STRUCTURE
BUILDING BLOCK 4

Jim Collins popularized the idea that great companies "get the right people on the bus, and the right people in the right seats, and the wrong people off the bus" before pointing that bus in a new direction.[1] There's good research that supports this maxim, and it strikes us as particularly true for senior leaders.

But when it comes to realigning an organization, generally we would argue that the right sequence is to begin with strategy, then move eventually to structure, and only then to staffing. It is better first to define the roles required in the new organization and then to fill those roles with folks who have the right skills and abilities for the job—whether or not they already work in your company.

That staffing should follow structure is Building Block 4.

How do you determine who are the right people for the new roles created in an organization alignment? That is largely a strategic question. If a firm shifts from a product-driven strategy to a customer-driven strategy, for example, the vice president with thirty years of product expertise may not be the right head for the new customer-centric division. If jobs are designed to align to the new organization, then talent can be aligned to the right jobs.

A public television station in the Asia Pacific region came under mounting pressure from subscription-funded competitors about the same time that customer viewing habits were changing with new delivery platforms such as smart phones. Their leaders could see a strategic change was needed. They hired consultants to perform a thorough marketplace analysis and then, with this data in hand, the new CEO, Andrew Martin, gathered the top two layers reporting to him and confirmed a new strategy and business model. They made the decision to integrate cross-functionally, and they set cost reduction targets.

Next, given the competing agendas of Martin's executive team, he reached out to the third organization layer—the next layer down—and engaged ten high-potential senior leaders to complete the organization alignment and to address the strategic and cost targets.

The team recommended a fundamental change to the organizational model to better enable it to deliver the right content, in the right place, at the right time. Their thinking demonstrated a significant departure from what had been an intractable mind-set at this state-owned enterprise that had preceded Martin's arrival. The team actually designed a structure that eliminated *nine* of their *ten* jobs and replaced them with substantially changed roles.

Martin was thoroughly impressed with the objectivity and hard work of this alignment team. Determined to ensure the new strategy drove talent placement decisions, he proposed that the entire senior leadership group—including his direct reports—apply for the new jobs as detailed in the new model.

Martin was firm in his resolve to realize the newly aligned organization, and his efforts were rewarded. At the same time, the livelihoods of the employees in the organization were preserved as much as possible as they were placed in roles for which they were best suited—even though they were not their old roles. All but one of the alignment team members found a position in the company. Roughly half of Martin's own reports were placed in the new organization.

The station was reborn. It grew its market share despite increasing competition. Profitability returned as well. Advertisers showed new interest in the broadcaster, and viewers at last were able to screen their favorite programs on multiple platforms.

Summary: Aligning Talent

Determining the names in the boxes before configuring the boxes is a missed opportunity to align individual strengths with organization strategy. Any time there is misalignment, results will fall below their potential. An organization alignment leader understands that staffing must follow structure.

Key Organization Alignment Concepts

We can add a new point to our list of keys for successful organization alignment. Remember that we have consolidated the list of concepts at the end of the book.

- Staff new jobs and jobs that change significantly because of the alignment process *after* they have been designed (staffing follows structure).

What You Can Do Now

To align an organization before staffing it means that you will ask current leaders to participate in the organization alignment process and that their decisions throughout the process may impact their own jobs. In our experience, most leaders relish the opportunity to be a part of organization alignment teams and have an extraordinary ability to act for the good of the overall enterprise. If one or more of your leaders do struggle to act in the company's best interest, know that there are techniques for helping those leaders engage positively in the process. Your change partner can assist in exploring those options.

Thinking about the organization challenge you selected at the beginning of this book, jot down your thoughts on the following questions based on the stumbling and the building blocks discussed in this chapter.

	Alignment leader responses	Change partner responses
If we could start from scratch, what are the right organizing choices to make?		
What people am I worried will leave or be disenfranchised if we change something?		
How can we do the right thing strategically and organizationally and still preserve and reengage our best people/talent?		

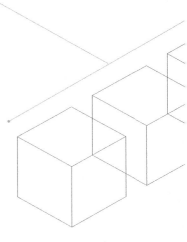

CHAPTER 5

HOW TO LEAD ALIGNMENT

We said earlier that organization alignment can and should be fast. So let's talk about *how* fast.

A group of leaders with an intimate understanding of the marketplace can systematically reconceive their organization in *three to five days.*

That's fast.

Yet incessant pressures to hit quarterly performance targets can undermine the best intentions to give some thoughtful time to organization alignment. If what leaders really want is just to get executives assigned to a new organizational chart, five days may seem like maddening overkill. They could be tempted to hurry the work along in order to get on with the "real" work before them.

"REAL WORK"
STUMBLING BLOCK 5

This temptation is Stumbling Block 5: underestimating the fundamental importance of organization alignment work to your enterprise and assuming it is not the "real" work of leaders.

Organization change is one of the most difficult imperatives of modern leaders. Most change efforts fail. New strategies are conceived but never deployed, values espoused but never widely internalized, technologies purchased but never fully utilized, processes redesigned but never implemented.

Think about times in your career when you have led or have been part of a change that took hold. What was different? Who was involved? How long did the process take?

If you are committed to bringing about lasting organizational change, then you need to focus on this task for a set block of time—at least three to five intense days. And those days only include the time with your executive team when you are in the conference room or off-site making the first sweeping pass.

However, when you reach this point you should not simply announce the new structure and all the changes in the reporting relationships and then turn back to your usual work. No, you will need to dedicate more time to this process as you begin to involve even more people in the change and guide the translation efforts when strategy must be rendered into detailed organizing choices and directors and managers strain against the sheer force of inertia that exists in a large organization. It is going to take some effort to integrate the change into the very fiber of the firm. The time commitment for leading the change at these lower levels can be quite significant for some weeks or months—maybe longer.

But you are an organization architect, and Rome wasn't built in a day.

BECOME AN ALIGNMENT LEADER
BUILDING BLOCK 5

The skill of organization alignment is one of the most valuable abilities of a leader who wants to see change flourish so that results can improve. An alignment leader is especially accomplished at getting organization change to take hold and become embedded in the organization for good. These leaders do not just don the hat of change leadership because they happen to head an organization in flux and have been dubbed a sponsor by savvy change agents. Rather, they have a distinct skill set. They do not necessarily stand in front of their group and motivate them charismatically, enticing them forward with their vision, stories, humor, and charm. Neither do they get behind their organization with their whips and cry, "Harder! Faster! Hit the target at all costs!"

What alignment leaders do is thoughtfully create and champion organizing choices that enable performance. They find formal ways to embody the yeses of their strategy as well as the nos. They have the fortitude to stand up for the deployment of new practices and also to identify and retire extant practices that are no longer strategically expedient.

This leadership work requires strength and tenacity, because the day-to-day roll of the organization can overwhelm alignments that are under way but not yet fully implemented. An alignment leader protects emerging processes and structures, even during the planning and transition phases, while at the same time keeping the current business running.

We once worked with a hundred-year-old diversified manufacturing and technology company whose divisions have learned to value organization alignment but strictly limit all strategic alignment sessions to three days total. High-level leaders come to important breakthroughs in these sessions and make significant decisions. Then they hand off their work to two or three directors and human resource practitioners to implement. These directors are bright. They are fast. But they are not effective, and how could they be? Two or three middle managers cannot mobilize an organization toward a new future on their own. That is the work of leadership. Because of their premature sense of completion, the leadership teams in this organization are soon back in the conference room working on the same problems.

The flaw in their process comes from failing to dedicate significant follow-up resources to their organization alignment efforts. Because they do not see alignment as their real work, they delegate implementation to a few individuals who might be able to pull off the staffing of new roles and get people hooked up in their new offices, but who in no way possess the influence necessary to overhaul work systems, behaviors, and other significant practices by themselves.

Alignment leaders have an alignment mentality. When they look at their institutions, they see all sides of the cube. They know that changes to one side can impact or even jumble all the other sides. Even though complex organizations will always be in motion, alignment leaders look for patterns that tell them the many facets are all working toward the same overarching objective—that of realizing the enterprise strategy. Their worldview is strategic alignment. When they see a problem, they ask what misalignments may be at the root. They speak often of organizing choices to drive systemic thinking. They understand that alignment is a tool to solve problems and that bringing other people along to think about alignment also generates enormous power in an organization. They know that inspired, innovative alignment produces the ability to deliver a competitive advantage.

Alignment leaders are passionate about optimal organization alignment to strategy.

Building Block 5 is to become an alignment leader. If you are the CEO, know that you are also the CAO (Chief Alignment Officer). The alignment of your enterprise to strategy is on you. If you are an executive, vice president, or division head, the alignment of your arm of the organization to strategy is on you. If you are a director or manager or any other type of leader, the alignment of your group to the enterprise strategy is on you. You are the alignment leader. This is your real work.

Steve Jobs acted as Chief Alignment Officer at Apple.

Throughout his career, he was an evangelist of putting easy-to-use technology in the hands of the masses. He loved simplicity. He wanted to "stretch the taste" of consumers with beautiful bright devices that were inviting and playful.[1]

It is well-known that he was often scathingly critical of his employees. He wielded the whip with an unbearable ruthlessness. He could be insulting and cruel. At the same time, he also had an uncanny ability to inspire people, to make them feel part of something revolutionary, to spur them to heights of achievement they did not think possible.

But these are not the traits that made him a great alignment leader. By the time he returned to Apple after leading NeXT and Pixar, he had learned that "the best innovation is sometimes the company, the way you organize a company."[2] He had a singular vision for high tech, and he believed that the means to achieve his vision had to be embedded in the capabilities of Apple. So he set about molding those capabilities. He became as visionary about organization design as he was about product design. Everything he believed came to be expressed in organization processes and structures. Apple grew to be the most valuable company in the world largely because of his organization architecting. "He became a manager," said Ed Woolward, the board member largely responsible for Jobs's return to Apple, "which is different from being an executive or visionary, and that pleasantly surprised me."[3] We daresay that Woolward's "manager" is our alignment leader—someone who not only talks the talk and walks the talk, but someone who also designs the talk into the organization.

Above all, Jobs wanted to have control of the full customer experience, extending from the experience in Apple stores, to the unpacking of a new product, to the use of both hardware and software. This strategy brought implications for alignment. Such integration requires extraordinary collaboration between specialties. When Jobs developed the Macintosh early in his career, he insisted that the case for the computer be designed first and then required the engineers to assemble the components to fit inside. He returned to Apple with the same philosophy on collaboration. As a result, Jobs instituted business processes aimed at "deep collaboration" and "concurrent engineering" across hardware, software, and devices. Workflows were not sequential—a product concept was not moved methodically through engineering, design, manufacturing, and finally marketing; rather, work on all these fronts occurred simultaneously. "Our method was to develop integrated products, and that meant our process had to be integrated and collaborative," Jobs said.[4]

User Experience

Side A: Work Processes

- *Distinctive store design with glass as a signature statement*
- *Concurrent Engineering: simultaneous product design across divisions*
- *Memorable product unwrap experience*

Side B: Structure & Governance

- *Linkage: extensive weekly meetings without formal presentations*

Side C: Information & Metrics

- *No divisional profit and loss targets*

Side D: People & Rewards

- *Collaborative hiring process focused on acquiring "A" players*
- *Apple U for transmitting critical company knowledge*

Side E: Continuous Improvement

- *Largest app marketplace (rigorous approval process and customer feedback)*
- *Annual worldwide developers conference*

Side F: Leadership & Culture

- *Ruthless about trade-offs*
- *Design thinking permeates company*

Figure 5.1: Apple's User Experience Capability and Organizing Choices

To make this happen, he linked people across organization boundaries through a series of weekly meetings. But Jobs despised slide decks
because they could disguise the presenter's lack of knowledge or muffle
his raw opinions and analysis. To keep all these meetings vital, Jobs dis-
pensed with formal presentations and instead insisted on long, lively debates where people from different perspectives owned up to and hashed
out their disagreements.[5]

To ensure he had the best talent for all these debates and decisions,
he set up a collaborative hiring process. He insisted on hiring only
A-players. Candidates for key positions met with top leaders in every
discipline, who then would get together to discuss the candidate's fit and
make the hiring decisions jointly.[6]

One of the most important workflows Jobs inaugurated was daily informal product reviews in the studio of Apple's design chief, Jony Ive.
Here Jobs would finger foam prototypes and discuss minute details of
product design. Thus, "there [were] no huge decision points," said Ives.
"Since we iterate[d] every day and never ha[d] dumb-ass presentations,
we [didn't] run into major disagreements."[7]

To deepen alignment across specialties, the Apple organizational
structure was very different from that of most other firms. There were
no product divisions that were their own profit centers. "We run one
P&L for the company," said operations head Tim Cook (who became
CEO after Jobs's death).[8] Thus, divisions did not compete against each
other for customers or worry about "cannibalization." This proved a huge
competitive advantage when Apple introduced the iPod and iTunes. Ri-
val Sony, rich in assets that could have given Apple a run for its money,
was undermined by their organization structure, which was divided into
profit centers that drove focus on product lines but hampered collaboration across these lines. Sony's music division and their consumer elec-
tronics division were never able to successfully join forces to compete
against Apple. Conversely, at Apple, all departments could celebrate a
sale, whether a consumer chose to download music through their iPod
or iPhone, or send emails using an iPad or MacBook.

Early after his return to Apple, in keeping with Jobs's dream of making his high-tech products playful, he decided to release the original iMac in five bright colors. He sped up the process of getting them to market by cutting out lengthy analysis work to affirm the value of this choice. "In most places that decision would have taken months," said Ives. "Steve did it in a half hour." But the move came at a huge cost, greatly increasing the complexity for the supply chain.

In fact many of Jobs's choices came at a high cost, and he was not unaware of this. To pay for top-notch design, playfulness, and an integrated customer experience, Jobs knew what to say no to. "Deciding what *not* to do is as important as deciding what to do," he said. "That's true for companies, and it's true for products."[9] His mantra was "focus."[10]

He insisted on getting "back to the basics of great products, great marketing, and great distribution."[11] At a product strategy session early after his return to Apple, Jobs's bewilderment and frustration at a plethora of redundant products reached a climax. He drew a two-by-two chart that divided the market into four segments—Consumer and Pro on one axis, Desktop and Portable on the other—and declared that Apple was to make one great product for each quadrant. He reduced product lines and operating system features. He got out of businesses extraneous to this core focus, such as printers and servers. He killed the Newton, an inelegant personal digital assistant. "By shutting it down," he said, "I freed up some good engineers who could work on new mobile devices. And eventually we got it right when we moved on to iPhones and the iPad."[12] He and Cook outsourced everything not essential to the customer experience. They streamlined the supply chain, enforcing a new discipline on suppliers, reducing inventory, and closing warehouses. Two months of inventory was sitting in warehouses when Jobs returned to Apple. Within eighteen months, he and Cook had reduced it to two days' worth.[13]

He also established Apple University to codify and analyze the company's most important decisions, such as the move to open Apple Stores. Executives discussed these cases with new employees as a way of passing on their most valued cultural assets.[14]

Jobs epitomized alignment leadership. We've depicted our discussion of Apple's capabilities and the organizing choices that produced them in figure 5.1.

Here are some other examples of master organization aligners:

- Muhammad Yunus, who created the Grameen Bank in Bangladesh to provide microenterprise loans to the poorest of the poor

- Madam C. J. Walker, who organized her massive network of hair-care sales agents into a decentralized system of civic activists

- James Madison, framer and defender of the United States' Constitution

- Taiichi Ohno, the creator of the Toyota Production System

- Jeff Bezos, founder and CEO of Amazon.com

For these individuals, being master aligners also included taking on a role as organization innovators. To achieve their strategies, they created novel organization designs that not only brought them unprecedented success in their own realm but also influenced the thinking and design choices of others.

Organization aligners do not just imagine a new future and inspire others to get excited about it. They actually figure out what it will take, step-by-step, choice-by-choice, to get there. Above all, alignment leaders are really skilled at the following:

- communicating the trade-offs implicit in new strategic direction

- formulating tactics to support strategic shifts

- organizing people to imagine new ways of working and linking with each other

- helping people act on trade-offs by taking on new responsibilities and adopting new processes while simultaneously ceasing old projects and routines

- recognizing and addressing how changes in one group will ripple through other areas of the business

- continually moving toward the change while keeping the current business running
- ensuring everyone in the organization is eager for and adept at this kind of M.O.
- discussing the organization in the language of choices; e.g., choices about staffing, decision making, resource allocation, rewards, policy making, and processes
- removing or eliminating organizing choices that get in the way of effectiveness and alignment (even when these organizing choices may seem to be unchangeable givens)
- funding a change all the way through to its full implementation
- making hard decisions about leaders whose capabilities do not fit the strategic direction

Cascading Organization Alignment

Let us say a bit more about how deep, penetrating organization alignment plays out and the sort of landscape over which an alignment leader must be comfortable presiding when the change is under way.

Once the institution's strategy has been modified or clarified, organization alignment efforts follow at two levels in sequence.

The first effort has to do with the aggregate alignment of the whole company or division. Because the scope is large, we call it *macro alignment*. Because it deals with questions of how the firm, division, or functional group goes to market and what organizational capabilities must stand behind the strategy, another term to describe this approach is *business model alignment.*

Macro alignment, or business model alignment, is the province of the organization's highest-level leaders. This work is very much about identifying and evaluating strategic capabilities—including what processes will have the greatest competitive impact and how best to group people to generate the most intense competitive focus. Far from being a distraction to weightier concerns, macro design is *absolutely* the real work of executives because it is essentially innovative and strategic in nature. Macro alignment often, but not always, involves structural change to the top three or four levels of the organization.

Macro alignment work can be accomplished very fast, involving only a week or two of discussions, or even as little as three to five days, as we cited earlier. Staffing adjustments to top-level jobs that result from macro alignment may take a bit longer, depending on the degree of change to existing jobs and the agility of the human resource and recruiting processes at getting people into new roles.

The second-effort pulse of organization alignment work—to move down the road in the new direction—involves organizing choices that are more detailed, more process-oriented, and that involve managers and contributors who actually perform the work that needs to change. The scope narrows to individual functions, processes, departments, and teams. It is often led by third- and fourth-level leaders in their new seats but can be carried out at any level. Because the focus is tighter, we call this *micro alignment*. Because it is in this pulse that the day-to-day work routines, jobs, decision-making realities, information tools, reward systems, and other policies really take on new forms, another term that describes this level of alignment is *operational alignment*. Micro design is *absolutely* the real work of mid-level leaders because it is essentially innovative and operational in nature.

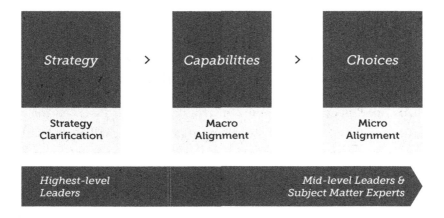

Figure 5.2: Cascading Alignment

Micro alignment is the bridge to classic continuous improvement practices such as Lean Six Sigma. The talents of the process designers in the organization come into play during this work. Micro alignment includes but is not limited to process improvement and metrics design, two of the most important arenas of continuous improvement. It also includes information systems design, job design, and more.

While *macro* alignment defines and enables new capabilities, *micro* alignment creates and aligns the DNA-level processes, structures, and practices that produce those capabilities. Micro-level efforts are the ones that actually change what an organization does. They re-sequence the genetic coding of the organization. Thus, micro design includes the hard work of making choices that also drive culture change.

For example, over the last decade, almost every organization identified the Internet as a channel that they needed to build capability in. Affirming that they wanted to use the Internet as part of their strategy and that they therefore needed cyberspace competence was all macro-level alignment. The actual creation of the department that was to manage the website, the processes they used, the roles in the group, the skill sets that were important, and how they linked up with the rest of the organization—that was all micro alignment. More recently, organizations are seeing the need to become proficient at integrating their offerings across channels—an omni-channel capability—and that is macro alignment. Making the organizing choices that build that proficiency is micro alignment.

> *Organization alignment efforts are not complete until micro alignment choices are put into action.*

This dual pulse of macro and micro alignment is essential for producing real change. If you instead face organization challenges by using the boxology attack and just rearrange the org chart boxes, you have not done the macro alignment very systematically, and you have not done *any* micro design. But it does take the fortitude of a strong Chief Alignment Officer and deputy alignment leaders to sustain the more systematic effort in order to get at the precious details of the routines and touch points that are the soul of a new strategy. Remember that this is the "real" work of leaders!

For example, we are excited by the work of the field leadership team at one of the US Midwest's largest energy utilities. They have effectively used organization alignment practices and approaches to adapt their complex service delivery organization to align with changing strategies and shifting demographics. Their field service group has long been organized geographically, a traditional structure that puts technicians in close proximity to customers. But the company's coverage needs are changing as rural areas grow into suburbs and once-vibrant cities shrink in population. Another impetus for change has been declining customer satisfaction scores, impacted significantly when service crews do not arrive on schedule. These scheduling delays are largely a result of resource imbalances when crews are redeployed for weather-related power outages. Utility leaders launched organization change with the aims of adjusting their crew distribution and finding a way to better adhere to their schedules.

The key organization innovation that emerged from macro (business model) design was to reorganize around the type of work that crews perform rather than their proximity to customers. Some groups are now responsible solely for scheduled service calls, while other groups are at the ready for unplanned emergencies.

This has been an enormous transformation in the delivery of field services. It has meant changing the footprint and the cost structure of the business. It has also required an unprecedented integration of the engineering, field crews, planning and scheduling, and customer service departments. The heads of these groups along with the senior vice president of distribution have shown all the qualities of alignment leaders that we described above. They've pulled together cross-functional macro (business model) alignment teams to plan the new organization and to identify how their new focus affects the strategic value of all work previously performed in the organization. They have formed micro (operational) alignment teams to engage in careful process design to ensure people know how the work will flow in the new structure and to see the impacts all the way through to new requirements of information systems and human resources.

The leaders at this enterprise have tackled some embedded assumptions about how to run and organize their field organization. Though their work is not yet fully implemented, they have demonstrated the insight and endurance required to reinvent how service is delivered in a changing environment. They understand that their organization design is of fundamental importance because it helps enable their customer services strategy.

Summary: Alignment Leadership

Alignment leaders have the vision and fortitude to guide their organizations through strategic change using a systemic, paced approach that involves employees at multiple levels to both envision the new organization and to stand it up via new processes, departments, measures, information systems, and people practices. They know that this is their real work. No short-cutting, no dodging, no delegating. The good news is that it's some of the most exciting work of all.

Key Organization Alignment Concepts

Our discussion about the fundamental work of organization aligners and the cascading approach to organization alignment gives us five new keys to leading a successful organization alignment effort:

- Build internal alignment leadership capability for creating organization alignment and managing change that really takes hold.

- Cascade organization alignment work down through the organization at a minimum of two levels of scope and detail. Macro (business model) alignment has the broadest scope and generates change in the business model and divisional/functional structures; micro (operational) alignment is more focused and brings about detailed change in processes, work groups, measurement systems, and people practices.

- Engage the leadership of the organization in the macro design process. In the end, they will be the ones to implement the new organization and adjust to the trade-offs.

- Engage those who do the work of the organization in the micro design process. In the end, they will be the ones who must do the work differently from before.

- Ensure leadership involvement is broad and remains committed to sponsoring a significant organization alignment effort from planning and chartering through full implementation.

What You Can Do Now

The success of an organization alignment effort at delivering the benefits of your chosen strategy hinges on your ability as an alignment leader not just to envision the change, but to massage it all the way down into the fibers of your enterprise or group. To deepen your change leadership skills or to build these skills in your team, a change partner can help.

Thinking about the organization challenge you have been focusing on, consider the following questions based on the stumbling and building blocks from this chapter.

	Alignment leader responses	Change partner responses
What roles will I need to play through organization transformation efforts?		
What competencies of an alignment leader are my strengths? What competencies need development? (See alignorg.com/ leading-the- design.)		
How do I help people accept the reality that organization transformation (or even mi- nor adjustments) require new thinking and behaviors?		
What can I do to help the organization stay focused on results now while we are designing how we will work in the future?		

	Alignment leader responses	Change partner responses
How do I help leaders speak the language of choices that drive alignment or misalignment?		
How will we cascade alignment choices from the macro level to the micro level?		
What are our plans to monitor and adjust the alignment of our organization's choices in an ongoing way?		

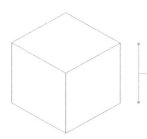

CHAPTER 6

HOW TO ACCOMPLISH GOALS USING ALIGNMENT

Many business leaders come to a realization at some point, for one reason or another, that they must increase their top-line revenues and cut expenses at the same time. When revenue growth or cost reductions are your imperative—and especially when both goals are your imperative simultaneously—organization alignment will help. Organization alignment offers potent concepts that will make it possible for you achieve this challenge and reach other financial goals.

GROW *OR* CUT
STUMBLING BLOCK 6

Let's begin by talking about how to approach cost cutting. The greatest myth about cost cutting is that it should be fair. Fairness dictates that leaders who must make reductions should require the same proportion of cuts from every division or department, such as 10 or 20 percent across the board. It's true that an equitable approach is less of a political headache than providing different targets to different divisions, functions, or departments. But a fairness methodology conflicts with a strategic methodology. Most people in an organization can sense this. A perfectly fair approach to cost cutting is not wise if it harms strategic interests. You can do great damage to the revenue machine of your company if you cut work that has a marketplace value just as deeply as you cut other parts of the business that are not as crucial to the customer. Following such a tactic, you risk slicing the muscle of your organization as well as the excess.

A good strategy can never be fair, because good strategy requires trade-offs. By definition, strategy requires prioritization. When it comes to making resourcing decisions, projects and processes with a greater competitive impact should garner higher priority. Those with lower competitive impact should feel a tighter squeeze. Thus, strategy is not fair.

If you devise targeted cuts, you can be gentle on your organization's competitive work and more aggressive on its non-competitive work. In this way, it may be possible to achieve savings without impacting revenue (or killing your people in the process). Indeed, if you properly value the competitive work in your organization by ensuring resources are directed toward it—by adding talent or tools or by improving process effectiveness—you can actually increase revenues even while you cut costs in other areas.

This reality flies in the face of Stumbling Block 6, the false belief that you cannot grow revenues and cut expenses at the same time. In fact, some organizations like GE have embraced the pattern of growing while becoming more efficient to the point that it is a way of life. It's tough (strategically), but it leads to focus through trade-offs.

RESOURCE *AND* REDUCE
BUILDING BLOCK 6

A multibillion-dollar sales division of a multinational conglomerate was tasked to grow by $200 million over an eighteen-month period. At the same time, they were required to cut costs by 10 percent. The sales executives gathered all kinds of data about their products, customers, processes, and touch points, hoping it would spark insights about how to accomplish both revenue growth and cost savings. But even with all the data before them, they were stumped.

So forty-five of the leaders from around the world met in a large conference room in Atlanta for an intense week of organization alignment discussions. The panels between three conference rooms were opened so that the group had kilometers of wall space for posting, mapping, and categorizing all of the division's work activities. These leaders understood that the competitive advantage of their organization lies primarily in its day-to-day work. If work doesn't change, results don't change.

The executives lasered in on the key work that they believed would create growth, and then they pinpointed other work where they could tighten efficiencies and perhaps even decrease their performance to par without impacting customers. That's right: they pegged the areas of the organization that could be average. That is where they planned to cut costs by eliminating or streamlining workflows and reducing head count.

Part of their approach involved making structure change to group competitive work more tightly together and separate it from non-competitive work. The mind-set required by the two workforces is different—one to strive toward differentiation and excellence, one to aim for extraordinary efficiency. Non-competitive work is not necessarily less important—many non-strategic tasks, such as payroll, sales administration, and network operations, are absolutely crucial for running the business. But non-competitive work tends to be more transactional in nature. It often feels more urgent as well. And herein lies the problem. If the same product expert who answers demanding administrative questions and labors to fill out complicated compliance paperwork is also responsible for helping to craft unique, integrated solutions for clients, the whole client experience—the competitive work—could easily fall apart. Prying apart these two different types of activities so different teams can perform them ensures that vital competitive work is not engulfed by less competitive tasks.

At the end of four long days—most of which went well into the evening—the forty-five global leaders had accomplished a substantial redesign. They had become intimate with all the work routines that made up their division around the world; they had sorted it, categorized it, and grouped it. That is how they were surgical in their cuts—work marked as "competitive" received more funding; work marked as "non-competitive" got tightened. For many of those executives, it was the first time they saw the truth: you can resource and reduce at the same time.

As their plans were implemented, new efficiencies did emerge as they had hoped, and they achieved both their growth and expense reduction goals. To boot, their work prompted other areas of the larger company to realign as well to support the solution-focused nature of their outcomes.

Building Block 6 is the alignment technique of resourcing strategic work to protect or stimulate growth while at the same time reducing or streamlining less strategic work to achieve cost savings.

You cannot perform the kind of surgical cost cutting we're talking about without knowing your trade-offs. All of the organizations that have been admired for their ability to grow over the last twenty years—Home Depot, Starbucks, Apple, and Amazon to name a few—have identified very significant trade-offs. Organizations that are not clear about their trade-offs have difficulty with surgical cost shifting or cutting. Since they say yes to everything, and they make reductions based on fairness, their people get overwhelmed and burnt out because they have too much work to do without enough resources.

For example, one big box retailer excelled for three decades by grabbing all the real estate they could get. Profits poured in, and the competitive race was to build more and more stores to capture the nearly unlimited demand. At the corporate offices, the real estate and merchandising divisions grew to be enormous. But as in most industries, things changed with the market downturn of 2008. Soon the company reduced the annual number of new stores by well over 90 percent and began the slow move to compete on customer experience rather than location and product. In other words, they chose to entice customers to drive further for new, robust, integrated product and service offerings.

With this new strategy, different work became strategically expedient.

Resources were moved from real estate to a customer experience group and other new strategic marketing teams. Projects were launched to enable omni-channel product fulfillment and customer data management. Aspects of the vast store operations empire were whittled and consolidated. This company made significant trade-offs during this transition: they made painful cost cuts in divisions that had been the workhorses of customer value for years in order to fund upstart teams with nascent but promising ideas about how to craft and deliver a new value offering.

The merchandising division of this retailer had once been the core of the business. Powerful towers within merchandizing had optimized decision making for their categories based on the belief that if the merchandising teams succeeded, so too would the entire enterprise. So they had independently designed their lines, sourced their products, and advocated raucously for space in advertising flyers and television commercials.

But with a new emphasis on the overall omni-channel customer experience, merchants became players in a much more expansive game, and the rules of the game were now devised by people with skills and experience that had previously either not existed in the organization or had not been viewed as strategic—groups who modeled, designed, and developed the new customer experience along with its pricing and marketing aspects. Merchant product categories were assigned roles to serve in the overall product mix, and some roles were promoted much more selectively than they had been in the past. As the new strategic jobs around customer experience began to consume resources in the organization, a trade-off had to be made—the company could not afford top talent in these new areas without deemphasizing the skills and pay of some of the merchandising groups.

It is easy to buy into exciting new strategies that promise to take you into the insanely awesome future. "We're going to differentiate ourselves by customer experience. Woot! Woot!" It is a downer to make the trade-offs. "We're moving heads and budgets from the juggernaut divisions of the past to fund the skunkworks and startups of the future." Ouch, that hurts.

When Steve Jobs returned to Apple, he eliminated 70 percent of the company's computer models and products. He enraged engineers who had put years of their lives into these products, and his cuts led to thousands of layoffs. But Jobs believed that good engineers applauded his decisions. He once reported that "he came out of [a] meeting with people who had just gotten their products canceled and they were three feet off the ground with excitement because they finally understood where in the heck we were going."[1]

At the same time, Jobs invested heavily in a very few initiatives that were selected with input from his most valuable employees. He held an annual retreat for them called "The Top 100." His biographer, Walter Isaacson, recounts the process:

> At the end of each retreat, Jobs would stand in front of a whiteboard . . . and ask, "What are the top ten things we should be doing next?" People would fight to get their suggestion on the list. Jobs would write them down, and then cross off the ones he decreed dumb. After much jockeying, the group would come up with a list of ten. Then Jobs would slash the bottom seven and announce, "We can only do three."[2]

Cost cutting is an organization alignment challenge because it impacts many systems that work together to contribute to organization results—among them work routines, job design, and staffing. When it is time to raise revenues or cut costs, decisions should be made that align with the strategic priorities. All work is not strategically equal.

Spending where you shouldn't prevents you from investing where you should.

Spans and Layers

Related to this discussion on reaching financial goals through organization design is the myth that it should be done by setting "guardrails" for the number of layers in the organizational hierarchy or the span of leaders' control. These guardrails, put forward by consulting groups or professional associations, are usually developed by studying industry averages or best-in-class practices.

While this information can be important input into setting staffing levels, we propose at least two cautions against relying solely on this research when establishing staffing targets.

The first is that benchmarks regarding spans and layers are most relevant when you are setting staffing levels for non-competitive processes—that is, work that is necessary but does not have a strong marketplace upside even when done exceptionally well. The performance goal of work with the designation of non-competitive is simply to be at par. Average is best. An industry average to gauge reasonable staffing levels makes a lot of sense in this case.

But you should be very wary of applying a benchmark to differentiating work where the goal of performing radically better than competitors may dictate the need for relatively lavish staffing. If you match the benchmark, you run the risk of killing the differentiation that you have proclaimed you wanted to build.

The other caution has to do with coordinating what work is phased out as a result of lower staffing levels. Leaders often let any such phasing out proceed of its own accord because they have faith that when they eliminate layers in the organizational chart or increase leadership spans of control, people who feel the increased workload will wisely and naturally eliminate tasks that are non-value added or of reduced competitive importance.

But this faith is misplaced if employees are not clear about the relative value of work or what the strategic trade-offs should be. If they do not know what work to eliminate, they may not eliminate any at all and instead pass it on to someone else. In this way the organization chart is like a square of jiggly jelly. If you squeeze the jelly from the top and the bottom, it is going to squelch out the sides, and if you squeeze from the sides, it is going to squelch out the top and the bottom. Increasing spans of control—giving leaders more responsibility—may soon result in more layers (for example, one firm created "senior technician" roles for technicians to fill as intermediaries for busy managers). Decreasing layers of the organizational chart may increase spans of control (for example, another company eliminated a layer of managers but then hired a couple of new directors to handle the additional workload when all the reports were reassigned to the next highest management level). The total head-count dollars are never reduced, just reapportioned.

The only way to stop the squelching is to change or reduce the work that is happening inside the square of jelly. But if people are not absolutely clear about the right strategic trade-offs, they may develop their own criteria about what to stop doing. "Most time consuming" and "easiest to put off" might become the guidelines for what work to stop. Yet these criteria likely describe your company's competitive work—work you would *not* want to eliminate.

When strategic differentiation is at stake, avoid applying guardrails for spans and layers. It is better to change the work side of the Rubik's Cube than just adjust the structure and governance side of the Cube. Save the benchmarks for processes with lower marketplace stakes.

The Role of Shared Service Functions in Cost Cutting

Another dynamic we see in many organizations is that executives fresh off discussions about surgical cost cutting and hungry to fund strategic new groups turn to the shared functions designed to enable the business and plead for help. Functional heads in Finance, IT, HR, and others feel duty-bound to contribute but often face a perilous professional dilemma we call the *functional imperative*. They feel a crisis about maintaining "best-in-class" functional standards. Their ranks have been populated by highly educated, highly competent specialists trained in first-rate methods of executing their work. Reduced labor dollars means reducing the frequency or the rigor of these processes simply because there are fewer people to carry them out. But functional leaders feel a loss of professional integrity when backing off from these standards.

Without a doubt, the reason best-practice functional methods have taken hold is that they have been proven effective by the educational institutions and professional organizations that steward the respective crafts. For example, top-notch selection processes do increase the odds that jobs will be filled by people who will succeed and therefore will retain these roles longer. But at some given level of staffing needs, these processes are impossible to execute comprehensively. Once a best-in-class process has taken hold in a functional group, it rarely seems to make sense to backtrack to lower professional standards.

For example, during the realignment of a finance function at one enterprise, the realignment team found that massive resources were dedicated to the monthly closing process in order to achieve 98 percent plus accuracy. However, when the realignment team interviewed business partners, they discovered that the business did not need or rely on such precision in their monthly analysis and planning efforts; a monthly accuracy record of 90 to 95 percent was good enough for business decisions. The quarterly close, on the other hand, needed to be 100 percent accurate. The accounting department struggled deeply with the idea of backing off from the precise monthly close. Only once the expectation of precision was shifted to the quarterly close could resources be reduced or re-channeled.

Both functional and business leaders must accept that sometimes the most advanced practices are out of alignment with the rest of the organizing choices due to the time or specialist talent they require. Building and housing high levels of functional expertise is not always cost effective. Extreme specialization can slow down competitive business processes because it is daunting to coordinate all the different people who must bring their rigorously thorough, laborious methodology or specialized knowledge to bear on an action or decision. When such a willing but unwieldy group of people are on hand to analyze, prepare, test, develop, ensure, monitor, check, conform, and comply, it becomes very difficult to act. Even if they are all Iron Chefs, sometimes there are just too many cooks in the kitchen.

Many functional groups fall into sheer and utter chaos because of misalignment (to their own dismay). They are not clear about how they hook up to enterprise strategy, and so their processes, structures, roles and responsibilities, and staffing are way out of line with what generates income in the marketplace. And they know it—people inside these functional failures often feel extraordinarily frustrated and cynical.

A valid way to cut costs is to tone down functional specialization in an organization. This is not a slight to professional integrity. It is a matter of strategic integrity. Alignment leaders are passionate about organization alignment, and ultra-strong functional specialization can be incongruent with marketplace requirements.

Summary: Reduce to Resource

Alignment leaders know that strategy is not fair. They have the insight and the language to talk about the relative strategic impact of all the work in the organization. They know how critical it is to lead the way in setting competitive work apart from the rest without sending the message that non-competitive work is any less important. When revenue growth and expense reduction are both on the table, their approach is to resource competitive work while reducing non-competitive work, and this response is one of the most handy tools of the trade. Strategic resource distribution like this is much more effective than across-the-board cuts. Alignment leaders put benchmark data about organization spans and layers in service of their own strategy, and they carefully evaluate the value of functional rigor against the needs of their own unique marketplace approach.

Key Organization Alignment Concepts

A discussion of the stumbling and building blocks associated with organization alignment and financial aims gives us another three keys to add to our list.

- Protect strategically vital work from becoming engulfed by the transactional work that characterizes so much of what must get done on a daily basis.

- Consider the strategic impact of work when making resourcing decisions. As a rule, generously allocate resources to strategic work with a goal of greater effectiveness, but manage non-competitive work toward greater efficiency.

- Guard against functional imperatives and professional standards that are misaligned to strategy and don't enable differentiation or compliance.

What You Can Do Now

Thinking about cost cutting in terms of organization alignment is a better approach than across-the-board mandates. If you want to extract resources strategically, start by understanding what work has the greatest impact in the marketplace. This approach will also help if your enterprise needs to continue to grow while you cut costs. Your change partner can help you frame the issues and the plan of attack for putting organization alignment in the service of growth or expense reduction. The following table contains some key questions based on the stumbling and building blocks discussed in this chapter.

	Alignment leader responses	Change partner responses
How do I ensure that economic pressures don't disrupt our organization's aligned organizing choices?		
What common myths do people in our organization hold that will make cost cutting or belt tightening a challenge?		
What approaches should we consider to cut costs (if needed) while enhancing our organization's ability to compete and grow?		
What structural imperatives are driving the use of resources that could be dedicated to driving work with a marketplace upside?		
What are potential functional imperatives (work that is resourced above or executed with greater rigor than the strategy would dictate) in our organization?		

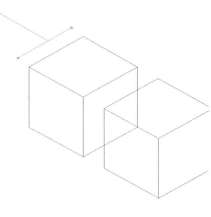

CHAPTER 7

HOW TO EMBRACE SIMPLICITY AND COMPLEXITY

We swim in a vast sea of clutter in our modern world. The marketplace is inundated with myriads of products with innumerable features that we do not know how to use and do not want anyway. We are constantly hit with messages aimed at turning our interest toward one of these products or another, but the messages themselves are often complicated or jarring. If we go out to shop, we visit enormous grocery stores and big box stores where the mega selection of products and the mega long lines tire us out. It is too much, and the way we often cope is to tune out. "The newest barriers to competition," says Marty Neumeier in his book *Zag: The #1 Strategy of High-Performance Brands,* "are the mental walls that customers erect to keep out clutter."[1]

What customers are shouting is, "Make my life simpler! There are too many choices! Save me time!" They are overwhelmed. So in vast numbers they retreat to the Internet to buy what they need; there they can easily search for it and find it, both new and used. They can compare prices online. At Amazon, they can purchase it with one click. We used to think two-day delivery was a deal, but now same-day delivery is increasingly available. The Internet along with other trends has re-sulted in the commoditization of goods and services. Customers buy on price. Small variations in features or branding are making less and less of a difference.

Most likely, these trends are not new to you. The world's companies have recognized these marketplace changes, and they are making stra-tegic adaptations. They are responding by differentiating themselves through increased simplicity and more personalization. They are offer-ing streamlined product designs, better user interfaces, kits, bundles, all-inclusive packages, mass customization, and specialty shopping.

Nearly without exception, the companies we work with are morph-ing their offerings to help customers bypass the clutter. They have rec-ognized that in the sea of choice that surrounds us, the offerings that are simplest *from the customer's perspective* are often the winningest. "One of the best ways to improve any experience," say Alan Siegel and Irene Etzkorn, authors of *Simple: Conquering the Crisis of Complexity*, "is to simplify it—to remove complications, unnecessary layers, hassles, or distractions, while focusing on the essence of what people want and need in that particular situation."[2] In fact, they say, "offering simplicity within a complex domain is likely to be so appreciated and valued by customers that it ends up being perceived as a luxury."[3]

Offerings that help people bypass the clutter are often called *solu-tions*. Solution-based offerings bundle goods and services together so the customer does not have to spend the time sorting through individual items, making choices about which are preferable, and assembling them for the job to be done.

Solutions are offered along a continuum of complexity as defined from the merchant's perspective. On the low-complexity end are simple kits or package deals—assemblies of multiple products or services, such as a movie DVD sold along with its digital version. On the high-complexity end of the continuum are true solutions, such as UPS's (United Parcel Service) supply chain service: businesses can outsource the transportation and distribution of their goods globally to "Big

Brown," which entices customers with their highly integrated global network and extraordinary transportation management capability.

High-complexity offerings that go even further in combating commoditization and clutter are called *experiences*. Experiences enrich the consumer purchase by amping up the sensations associated with the use or consumption of some aspect of the good or service offered. According to B. Joseph Pine and James H. Gilmore, authors of *The Experience Economy*, experience-based offerings use goods and services ultimately to "engage customers, connecting with them in a personal, memorable way."[4] One example is an "eatertainment" restaurant like Hard Rock Café where the food may not even be the centerpiece of the evening. Other examples include immersive eco-tourism packages, the personalized experience of custom-designed apparel (e.g., custom Converse sneakers), the fun of a full day of family shopping at an Ikea, the style and sensibility of a Tesla electric car, or the rugged outdoor ambience of a Cabela's outfitter. These offerings appeal to customers because they bring products, services, and even emotions together in one tidy adventure.

Amazon achieved retail dominance because Jeff Bezos insisted on making the full online shopping experience as simple and convenient as possible. The company reduced barriers by making it easy to select, pay for, and receive products. By facilitating online reviews of products, making personalized recommendations to customers about what products they might be interested in, displaying what other customers with similar browsing histories are buying, and giving sales rankings, they help customers make choices and find what meet their needs best. "We don't make money when we sell things," says Bezos. "We make money when we help customers make purchase decisions."[5] By inventing the 1-Click ordering process, they made it simpler for customers to make purchases. By telling customers which day they can expect their packages to arrive, and by giving reliable two-day delivery free to Amazon Prime subscribers, they made the wait for orders easier. Brad Stone, Jeff Bezos's biographer, predicts Amazon will continue to integrate vertically because of the need to control the full customer experience. "Will Amazon one day own its own delivery trucks?" Stone asks. "Yes, eventually, because controlling the so-called last-mile delivery to its customers can help fulfill [the] vision and improve the company's ability to meet the precise delivery promises it relishes making to customers."[6] If plans hold for the company's recently announced delivery drones, within the next few years they will take charge of the last-mile delivery in innovative Amazon style as well.

THE SIMPLICITY COMPLEX
STUMBLING BLOCK 7

Here is the rub: though organizations everywhere are adapting their *strategies* for these new marketplace realities, they are slower at adapting their *organizations*. Strategies toward simplicity and integrated experience are far ahead of most organizations' abilities to deliver offerings that are heightened in these new ways. *Stumbling Block 7 is in the way: the simplicity complex.* It's the impulse to absorb complexity for customers without adding or changing organization capabilities.

ABSORB COMPLEXITY
BUILDING BLOCK 7

The unpleasant truth is that creating experiences heightened by elegant simplicity, engaging entertainment, or active participation in an event means absorbing complexity on behalf of the customer. It means orchestrating touch points in a new, highly sophisticated way. Alignment leaders must recognize that their organizations cannot get simplicity and integration for customers without taking on some complexity.

Steve Jobs said, "It takes a lot of hard work . . . to make something simple, to truly understand the underlying challenges and come up with elegant solutions."[7] Likewise, it takes a lot of hard work—a new kind of work—to assemble a solution or stage an experience.

We are speaking especially to alignment leaders at large firms whose offerings of the past were delivered by organizations geared toward product innovation, manufacturing excellence, or marketing brilliance. We warn you that you cannot hope to become a supplier of solutions or experiences by simply tacking on these new responsibilities to current units. Doing so will increase the complexity of the unit, yet the broader focus will hamper your ability to deliver solutions to the marketplace that appear simple and seamless. You may also need to reconsider cross-organizational choices such as P&L ownership, compensation schemes, and cross-division processes where groups deliver outcomes jointly to customers rather than interim deliverables to the next-in-process recipient.

Strategic change of the magnitude we are speaking cannot be executed by reshuffling a few boxes or slapping on a couple of new processes. Absorbing complexity for customers necessitates increased integration across your business. Say you are Target and you want to create an offering that will appeal to new college students who are shopping for dorm room supplies. You identify the value of a pre-bound selection of goods. You select the right items for the bundle: a bucket, cleaning solutions, a laundry bag, a microwave-safe bowl, and a cookbook for quick meals. Making this package available requires integration across product categories to select all the products, ensure they are available, and price the bundle right. Then your supply chain must absorb the complexity of picking and shrink-wrapping these items.

Any institution intent on enhancing their offering by smoothing out marketplace intricacies must realign their whole system of internal routines and other organizing choices.

If you hope to become a complexity sponge for your clients, you must develop new complexity-absorbing capabilities.

No one really wants to talk about this brutal reality, because no one likes more complexity. That is why the Rubik's Cube analogy makes people groan with appreciation: the complexities of their own organizations make them want to toss their scrambled cubes aside and find something else to solve that is more manageable.

The folks who make up the workforce crave simplicity at work just as much as consumers crave simplicity in what they purchase. But it is an irrefutable reality that someone along the value chain is going to have to do new work to absorb added complexity. *Enter Building Block 7: Absorb complexity for your customers by investing in new capabilities for your organization.*

Consider the case of a diversified manufacturing and technology company that has long been a marketplace leader in the dental supplies industry; we will call them Dentabrand. They have been masters of product innovation, and their strong technical edge has given them a solid foothold at the front of the pack. They produce the whitest, longest-lasting, fastest-setting fillings, crowns, composites, cements, and adhesives in the industry. These materials have gotten so good through continued innovation over the years that they have almost become too good. The aesthetic materials are far whiter than customers need. The cements are the most durable, the most flexible, and have the greatest viscosity. They outlast every other part of the tooth and the restoration. Despite these amazing product features, Dentabrand is finding that their products are commoditizing. Practitioners do not see any measurable value in the additional innovations they are developing—at least that the customer is willing to pay for. To many, a filling is a filling is a filling (and thus a cement is a cement is a cement).

To combat the slippage in market share, Dentabrand is moving to differentiate themselves by increasing the value they add to a dental procedure as a whole rather than to individual products. They plan to provide integrated solutions to dentists that are bundled by the job to be done—a kit for a filling or a crown, for example. This is a promising solution-based strategy because their product portfolio is so massive they can bring nearly everything to the table.

Dentabrand's challenge now is to realign their organization to produce new capabilities and to find ways to change how customers think. They need to redeploy money, talent, and time from the work that has been their strategic bedrock for decades. Let's think through some of the significant pain points:

- In the past, the cements product leader was tasked to improve the cement each year. But since it has gotten so advanced, does it really require the same rate of improvement? Could the firm call it good enough for the next decade and refocus those resources on improving other products that would enhance the overall solutions (the jobs to be done by the dentist)? If the company redeploys cement product leaders to other products, what happens if they do not like their new career trajectory? They may risk losing people with hard-won expertise.

- What about the scientists who have proprietary knowledge of cement technology? Will the firm's competitive edge be damaged if they leave for a company where there is more action around dental cement?

- What about the sales force? They have learned to push products by talking up technology enhancements; what happens when the cement does not improve for a few years? How will the cement sales folks get their bonuses if there is no new cement?

- What about new vendor partnerships? If the firm seeks to add bibs and masks to their offering bundle, they will need to negotiate with new offshore suppliers. These products are likely to be low margin. How will the company fund the investment in the new vendor management capabilities? Further, how will they explain to the investment community that their margins are going down due to the margin-diluting products being added to the solution even though sales should be going up?

- What about the financials? Volume has been shrinking even though profitability has been rising for this company. So leaders have set goals to increase volume while maintaining a unilateral margin rate of 30 percent in all markets for all products. That is what the new procedure-based solution strategy is for—to drive up volume. But can they maintain such high margins when assembling their goods into a package? Some goods in that package may never command a 30 percent margin. Can the company live with that? Can they adjust financial goals to allow for an overall solution margin rather than holding each product line accountable? Can they redesign compensation packages so that the margin hit taken by products price-sacrificed for the overall bundle does not disadvantage the people behind these products?

- How will the company distribute these new solutions? Their current distribution partner prints a catalog that could conceivably offer the package, but they have no incentive to promote Dentabrand over any others, and there is no capability there to teach practitioners how to select among these new packaged offerings. Dentabrand needs to invest in helping their partner sell in a new way, or they need to invest in a different channel to go to market if they hope to show practitioners the advantages of the new way of purchasing supplies.

The moment a company that has grown up around a product focus decides to go to market for the first time with a solution package is the moment they will need to realign metrics, performance goals, training priorities, hiring practices, and compensation policies. Things are going to get more complex, at least for a while, and this is especially true if they don't make trade-offs. If you say yes to a solution-based offering, you are wise to say no to some other aspect of your organization—perhaps product-oriented sales jobs, financial targets, and incentives.

If you fail to accomplish this kind of alignment, you will be eaten alive by small companies built from the ground up to deliver solution- and experience-based strategies.

Consider co-author Kreig's experience with a bathroom remodel. He and his wife, Sherry, had hired contractors before for other home improvement projects and been less than thrilled with the results. Workers had traipsed in and out of their home for months, leaving their materials and their mess in between weeks-long absences. Sherry, truly a saint by everyone's account, found that even her gentle temper teetered when a window replacement project was still unfinished at the six-month mark.

So hoping for a different kind of experience, the Smiths began their next project with a visit to a home improvement store. They browsed through some interesting tile and millwork, but they wanted help putting a complete bathroom together, and they said so. The retailer could not oblige.

So with some hesitation they called several local contractors for bids, and the winner presented a service that was entirely different from any of the others. *Three* guys showed up for the consultation: a sales guy, a plumbing guy, and a tile guy. After listening to Kreig and Sherry talk about what they had in mind, they poked around the existing bathroom and took measurements. They promised that a designer would accompany them to visit fixture showrooms, and they pledged to clean up completely every night. They made good on their promises, and the bathroom remodel was a revelation.

How do large organizations create this kind of interface with clients? How can they hope to integrate across their massive girth to deliver an experience that is satisfying and appears seamless? How do they overcome the organization legacy left behind from old strategies—mind-sets and routines and systems and practices geared toward very different outputs?

They do it through organization innovation and alignment: systematically considering the full set of organization choices that deliver capability. We suggest a principle to keep in mind:

Simplicity for the customer first; simplicity for the organization second.

Combating Complexity with Trade-offs

When your firm moves to more integrated offerings, the degree to which the new value being offered is different from your current offerings is the degree to which the organization will need to take on new forms and routines. This presents a *capability challenge*, which we have just discussed, as well as a *complexity challenge*.

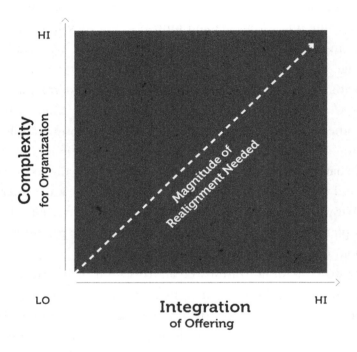

Figure 7.1: Absorbing Complexity

As you increase the range of integration that you offer for your customers, you will need to develop new skills and systems to effect this integration (fig. 7.1). However, it is important to avoid adding new skills and systems without also eliminating those that supported older strategies on their way out. The way to combat such crowding—to avoid creating a vastly more complex organization—is by making trade-offs. You as organization alignment leader must find a way to make trade-offs that will reduce clutter in your organization. *Simplic-*

*ity for the organization comes when leaders are crystal clear in identi-
fying and communicating trade-offs.*

When Steve Jobs killed 70 percent of Apple's models and products on
his return to the company, he was making trade-offs and reducing organization complexity. When Ikea limits the renewal rate of their product
range—the rate at which new items replace items offered in the past—
they are also making trade-offs to protect logistical efficiency and reduce organization complexity.[8]

As you offer your customers greater integration, you can add organization capability and combat organization complexity, keeping things
clear and focused for your workforce, by taking the following actions:

- Clearly delineate the capabilities essential to deploying your
  new strategy.

- Decrease the range or the novelty of your products.

- Clarify and communicate trade-offs to increase simplicity
  where possible.

- Shift resources from work that is no longer (or never was)
  strategically vital.

- Create new linkages or groups that allow collaboration for
  orchestrating customer touch points (like the big box retailer
  who created a new "customer experience group" to design
  seasonal offerings).

- Fill leadership roles with people who are exceptional at thinking
  beyond their spheres and reaching out across boundaries. Past
  leadership competencies may no longer fit future needs.

- Create metrics and incentives geared toward overall performance
  and avoid punishing people and products that play a supportive role.

- Maintain systems and business rules for collecting customer
  information, storing it, and making it available at strategic
  touch points.

- Train people in new ways of assembling solutions, selling in teams, connecting with customers, and so on (like Disney associates treating customers as "guests").

Summary: Mastering Simplicity

Organizations moving to more integrated product offerings and services have a huge challenge. They need strong alignment leaders who can help them build new strategic capabilities while keeping a rein on unnecessary organization complexity. This challenge requires having a firm grasp of all six sides of the organizational cube and manipulating them deftly to align and realign the facets throughout such momentous strategic shifts. But by phasing out the processes and practices associated with now defunct strategies, alignment leaders can make room for new ways of doing business.

Key Organization Alignment Concepts

A discussion about the complexity challenges presented by recent marketplace trends sheds light on keys presented in earlier chapters:

- When your strategy is moving toward delivering ever more complex solutions, build new strategic capabilities for integration and linking.

- Ensure that you articulate strategic trade-offs to minimize organization complexity for employees.

- Before building an organization that can deliver a complex customer solution strategy, be sure you understand the costs— both literal and organizational—of building the capabilities necessary to absorb complexity. It is going to be a lot of work and take a lot of time.

- Understand and address the touch points between the capabilities you are building to overcome complexity. Think through ways of linking people whose work is interdependent across boundaries.

- Consider how all organizing choices will contribute to greater integration, including work processes, decision making, structure, metrics, and other management systems.

- Unite the organization around a clear and targeted customer experience.

What You Can Do Now

If your strategy has moved toward more integrated offerings as a way of enhancing life for your customers, you are likely facing the huge organization design challenge of coping with the resulting complexity. If you have not already, you will want to align all systems toward delivering an integrated solution or customer experience. Your change partner can guide you through part or all of the effort.

As you consider ways to address your organization challenge, answer the following questions based on the stumbling and building blocks discussed in this chapter.

	Alignment leader responses	Change partner responses
What integrated offering, if any, will create distinctiveness in our business (e.g., a solution, an experience, or a service)?		
What integration or linkage capabilities do we need?		
What other capabilities will we need to consider investing in to ensure we can deliver the solution or experience or service we are hoping to?		
If we cannot make the full investment now, how can I guide the organization to gradually build out the capabilities needed to enable integration and simplicity for the customer?		

	Alignment leader responses	Change partner responses
What trade-offs will we consider making to fund the capability build-out that is needed (at least until the up-side of our new strategy starts to deliver)?		
How will we describe the targeted customer experience in a way that unites everyone in the organization?		

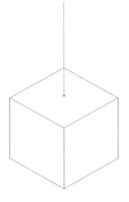

———•———

CHAPTER 8

WHEN TO ALIGN

In previous chapters we discussed the reasons why leaders sometimes do not involve enough people in realignment efforts, and we noted that commitments to realignment efforts have a tendency to fray before full implementation.

On the other hand, we have also seen many leaders sponsor thoroughly systematic, high-participation realignments. They understand the advantages of bringing a full range of organization systems into harmony with changing strategies and of involving scores of talented people. Their commitment to the initiative remains enthusiastic through full implementation.

■ ONE AND DONE
STUMBLING BLOCK 8

But sometimes these leaders who are strongly committed to alignment believe that such initiatives can or must be singular or rare events. They feel that organizational expediencies make revisiting the design out of the question—that there is not going to be enough time, money, or energy to put the institution through a similar effort ever again.

Therefore, they direct their alignment teams to get the design right, this time, once and for all.

What we have here is Stumbling Block 8: the one-and-done mentality that if we nail our organization design this time, we will never have to realign again.

In response, know this: there is no perfect organization design, and even if there were, no design is perfectly aligned forever.

The Imperfect Organization

All organization designs, no matter what their strengths and how well they facilitate your current strategy, also have inherent weaknesses. You will feel them sooner or later once the design is implemented and external realities drift from the current state. No design can be everything for every person in the organization or ideal for each and every endeavor you pursue.

For example, take an organization structured around a functional rationale, where the primary groupings bring people together based on their technical expertise: research and development, engineering, operations, marketing, finance, etc. This structure emphasizes functional specialization and control. But the trade-off here is that it is less likely to enable the development of cross-organizational capabilities needed to offer solutions and experiences, as we discussed in the last chapter.

Likewise, a firm organized around product lines encourages strong product expertise and clear accountability for success; employees are deeply knowledgeable about their product offerings. The trade-off in this case is less intimacy with customers and their customers' entire range of jobs-to-be-done.

Customer structures, in which employees are organized by customer segment, fare better at satisfying customers and scoring higher margins, but the transfer of product knowledge is hampered across boundaries and workers tend to lose strategic focus as they try to be too many things to too many people.

The structure you ultimately settle on should be one that best enables your unique strategy. That said, it is important to be aware of the weaknesses of the structure you select. When you recognize the downsides, you can develop mitigating tactics, as we discussed with Stumbling Block and Building Block 2, and find ways to capitalize on the strengths of the design.

The Aligned Organization That Falls from Grace

Though a carefully selected set of organizing choices—even given their imperfections—will ably support your strategy for a time, as performance evolves and the marketplace changes, you will eventually find its limits.

The set of upsides and downsides that characterize your organization have an expiration date.

Changing external conditions will render your organizational model obsolete sooner or later. For example, as we saw in the last chapter, customers are increasingly drawn to solutions that bundle many products and/or services together or that offer robust experiences to entertain or educate them in all-in-one packages. These trends signal a whole new kind of economy—dubbed the "Experience Economy" by Pine and Gilmore.[1] Upstart entrepreneurs will continue to innovate with technology and disrupt the marketplace as Google and Amazon have done over the last few decades. And a host of other conditions will present themselves that require your organization to respond by remaking itself.

Figure 8.1: Change and Realignment

The myth of long-lasting organization perfection would be possible if the following were true:

- *Your business model never changes in order to stay competitive.* In industry after industry, companies are learning that they must differentiate themselves through the full customer experience. Just as HP has repeatedly reinvented itself—morphing from a product focus (first instruments, then calculators, then computers and printers) to an enterprise and cloud computing service model—so other companies that endure over time have adapted to a changing world with new offerings and new organizations that support those new offerings.

- *Your company never undergoes a merger, acquisition, or divestiture.* These events raise fundamental strategic questions. Sometimes an acquisition is purely to obtain the technology, product, talent, or market access of another organization. But sometimes an acquisition, divestiture, or split results in a fundamental change to the value proposition and thereby calls for realignment.

- *You never expand into new markets.* Moving into a new geographical region can raise questions about how to deliver products and provide service to customers who live in a part of the world where you have no infrastructure. Likewise, moving into a new product arena requires new capabilities for sourcing, distribution, pricing, merchandising, marketing, and more.

- *Your firm never expands sales into new channels.* Companies are not just finding multiple pathways to interact with consumers; they are also using customer information from all those channels to personalize the customer experience based on their lifestyle and purchasing behaviors. Integrating these channels and this information is new for most organizations.

- *Your company is never affected by technology change.* Outdated technology often means outdated work processes, and product innovation unfailingly requires new ways of producing, delivering, and selling.

- *Competitors don't change the value they are offering to your customers.* Competing in the marketplace guarantees you will always have some level of turbulence because by definition competitors are constantly changing the very nature of what you have to deliver to stay in the game. Ideally, you will hold your ground well ahead of your competitors, but they will always be hoping to leapfrog you if they can.

The truth is that organizations face these realities incessantly because the marketplace is so volatile. As long as there is a global marketplace and exploding technological progress, the need for formalized and on-going organization alignment efforts will continue unremitting as well.

DESIGN FLUIDLY
BUILDING BLOCK 8

The truth is that good alignment leaders—strong strategists that they are—continually evaluate changes in both marketplace dynamics and organization performance to determine when strategies and thus organizing choices must be modified. *Thus, Building Block 8 is to design fluidly for continuous organization alignment.*

Such leaders are shrewd at seeking out marketplace signals through a variety of means. They put their hands on the pipeline of information streaming from their market analysis groups—market research, strategic planning, business development, consumer intelligence, and the like—sieving it for indications that a change is in order and saturating key strategic discussions with this information.

They gauge organization performance by examining traditional financial metrics, but they also review employee engagement surveys to monitor the pulse of the organization's talent. Sometimes they use organization health assessments to detect misalignments in the workplace. These assessments are specifically designed to provide data about the degree to which employees understand the strategy and its trade-offs as well as to gauge their perceptions about how well the systems in the organization enable them to execute the strategy.

As leaders identify necessary strategic changes or declining organization performance, they respond by launching organization changes. If necessary, they take the plunge on major transformations when triggered by one of the legitimate reasons we discussed above. But short, targeted adjustments can keep an organization on track between major strategic shifts. By making incremental change on a constant basis, leaders can lengthen the time between large-scale realignments.

An organization needs to move like an amoeba, with new or existing divisions throwing themselves outward in new directions, flowing away from nonstrategic products and projects, the whole reshaping itself steadily. We are often asked by clients to help them design an organization that will be flexible and adaptable. Ongoing and regular alignment checks along with short, targeted design adjustments yield an organization that is constantly renewing.

The amoeba model is preferable to a model where change happens infrequently, in large, lurching efforts. While it may be impossible to entirely avoid periodic leaps to adapt to rapidly shifting markets, it is better for change to be organic and flowing. Continuous organization alignment should feel natural and comfortable, just one of the ongoing activities that come with running a company. People should be able to continue to run the business while engaged in alignment; indeed, alignment should feel like the everyday innovative work of responding to changes in the environment and in the customer.

Thus, rather than coveting a perfect design that never has to change again, alignment leaders should be helping their organizations strengthen the muscle of ongoing organization alignment.

Organization Innovation

That said, when organizations get behind—which can and will happen—they can leverage their organization alignment skills as one way of producing the innovation necessary to regain traction.

When Mike Abbott took on the bankcard group at GE Retail Consumer Finance in 2002, his task was to revitalize GE's bankcard business. The core business for many years had been private-label credit cards—cards branded by single retailers such as major department stores and gas stations for use exclusively at those outlets. But the team wanted to expand. They considered relaunching the general purpose bankcard—cards identified by payment network such as Visa or MasterCard that are widely accepted throughout the economy. But, searching for a stronger competitive advantage, they created the dual card instead.

Dual cards are labeled both by the retailer and the payment network and can be used as general purpose cards, but they provide an advantage to retailers because they supply robust customer information. They also build brand loyalty by featuring benefits that can be used only at the retailer. So, for example, using a Visa branded by a major discount chain saves the consumer 1 percent at that chain and $.05 per gallon at the chain's gas stations, but it can also conveniently be used at a restaurant or auto body shop—and even earn cash back on those purchases as well.

The primary competitive advantage that GE would gain in issuing these cards was two-pronged: they could leverage their large existing database of private-label customers to promote the cards, and they could replicate their established acquisition method to gain new customers as well. GE had long marketed private-label cards at the point of sale, right at the checkout line, while issuers of general purpose cards relied largely on direct mail campaigns. The industry average cost of acquiring one general purpose card account through direct mail was $175. GE could do it at the point of sale for less than $10.

Developing dual card partnerships with existing and new retail clients was a huge change in strategy that required new organization capabilities. Abbott and his team spent three years building the foundation for the business, investing $20 million in systems and $100 million in marketing.

By 2005, dual cards were showing great promise, but the team competed internally with the private-label team for resources and management attention. The two product groups stood side by side, their leaders reporting to the head of Retail Consumer Finance. Abbott believed the division could never reach its full potential as long as these two product verticals operated independently.

So he recommended that his fledgling dual bankcard group be merged with the core private-label business. And here is where the company leveraged organization alignment to gain a competitive advantage: the top-level general managers were organized into client teams focusing on major accounts, and each team managed the products offered through that client (fig. 8.2). "This was the complete polar opposite of what you would do in a traditional bankcard business, because you would never put the distribution above the product leader," says Abbott.

Abbott took the leadership of a new marketing group, which stood alongside these client teams. It was also divided into client teams that partnered with the general managers. They were connected by goals and metrics that guided the performance of all the client's products, and together they were mandated to transform the overall retail consumer finance business into a growth engine for GE.

To help drive this growth, the creativity of the marketing teams needed to be unleashed. Their most valuable work was creating methods to integrate the private-label card and the bankcard together at the point of sale, to leverage that distribution channel as GE's most distinctive advantage. Abbott gathered his leadership group to take a good look at all the work the marketing teams were doing and to ferret out tasks that could be unloaded from their plates to open up more space for the competitive work.

For instance, the larger marketing teams focusing on the biggest retailers each had their own direct mail team. "Direct mail was an execution function," says Abbott. It was a necessary function but did not have significant differentiating impact. "The leaders, because non-competitive work must get done, spent all of their time worried about execution errors, operation issues, and Six Sigma. They didn't have the time or they just chose not to spend the time on strategic issues." So to amp up work of true strategic value, "we found all of the non-competitive work—the execution components—and we centralized it and made it much more efficient. It actually gave the marketing teams more time to do the things that mattered most."

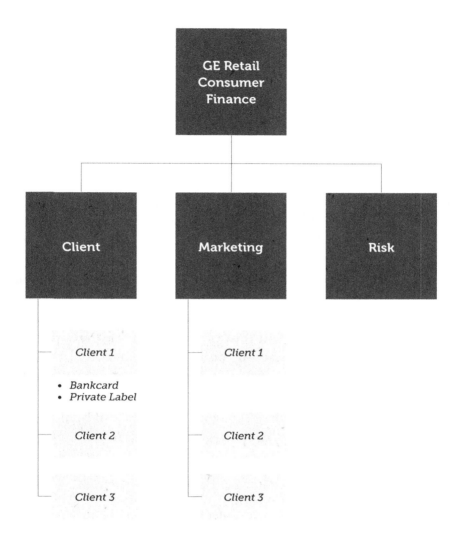

Figure 8.2: GE Retail Consumer Finance

Each marketing client team created unique approaches for giving end-user consumers private-label advantages with general purpose convenience. One launched the first branded Discover card and another the first branded American Express card. A third client team developed a cross-brand loyalty program for a major clothing retailer that accumulated points redeemable across all their brands. "Had we not pulled the direct mail team out of that marketing team—forgetting the efficiency games we'd played—they would never have had the organizational focus or time for this creativity."

"When you take the operational pieces away you expose everything," says Abbott. "There's no place to hide. At the time, people inside of GE loved to focus on the process. That's something that was rewarded and talked about. GE didn't necessarily reward the strategic growth accomplishments. You almost had to take away the process work and leave nothing for them to do." At first, he had to keep reminding the marketing team leaders that they were no longer responsible for solving process issues with shared execution work like direct mail. But once they internalized their new freedom to focus on new strategic programs, their creativity exploded. By the time Abbott left after eight years and at the height of the recession, net income at GE's Retail Consumer Finance division had quadrupled. Three years later it had doubled again, and the business was in the process of being spun off by GE.

GE Retail Consumer Finance is an example of using organization alignment to deliver a competitive advantage. By turning the traditional industry structure on its head—by positioning product teams underneath client-focused teams in the organizational chart—the new model enabled a new strategic capability: the know-how to integrate and sell multiple credit card products at the retail point of sale. By carving out non-competitive work from key strategic marketing teams, they saved money and freed the human energy to develop new, innovative products.

"Organizations are just legacies," says Abbott, who now heads Isis, a mobile payment venture of wireless carriers Verizon Wireless, AT&T, and T-Mobile that vies against Google Wallet and others for a piece of the digital wallet business. "They are often just legacies left over from what was once a successful approach. They don't align to the future state of what you are doing. It can be as simple as determining that the most important thing to you right now is a customer-sensitive approach, meaning you're serving a B2B (business-to-business) channel, so you organize around those B2B channels like we did at GE. Or it could be that the end consumer is the most important thing and you have to organize around product. You have to change." Abbott took his experience with realignment to Isis and now regularly involves his new team in realignment efforts to keep the growing organization in line with its rapidly changing strategic priorities. "I would say that the organization has to align to the future state," says Abbott. "More often than not, what you find is organizations are aligned to where you've been, not where you're going."

Continuous Organization Alignment

To keep their organizations aligned to the future and not the past, some CAOs (Chief Alignment Officers) and other alignment leaders embed a review of their organization's alignment into their strategic planning processes. Most business planning articulates the institution's current strategic intent and ensures it flows through the budgets and spending plans. But alignment leaders are alignment minded. They know that strategies determine needed capabilities, which in turn can be developed through organizing choices.

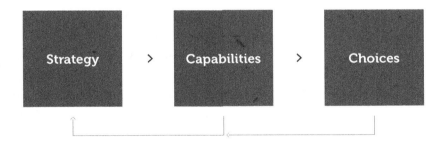

Figure 8.3: Continuous Organization Alignment

So as part of the business planning cycle, they want to know about the congruence of their overall organization to strategy. They want a full systems check. They ask profit center leaders to conduct alignment assessments to explore the need for organization change. This review helps leaders identify and invest in holistic capability building in addition to the more traditional costs of plants, systems, and equipment. When outputs like these are part of the business planning methodology, executives can help their institutions be more aware of organization degradation and can prioritize and schedule adjustments to even out the cadence of major change. In joint planning sessions, they can look at the big picture together to decide when change is a good idea and when it is better to stand pat.

We recently received an email from one of our clients evidencing this thirst for ongoing alignment checks. She said, "We would like to see one of the primary deliverables from [our next] project be a repeatable process that we can fold into our long-term planning process, instead of having it as a one-off type of project." Companies like this want their profit center leaders to develop continuous alignment know-how. For example, GE has historically used what they called Session C meetings to evaluate organization and leadership performance and to engage in succession planning. Abbott Laboratories holds an annual process called the Organization Health Assessment. At Tyco it's the Organization Leadership Review, or OLR. And on and on.

Our colleague Adam Anderson calls this marriage of strategic planning and organization alignment *liquid design*. The term indicates that large enterprises can and should be in a constant state of change as divisions or groups within divisions are continuously renewed and realigned. In this approach to planning, profit center heads are masters of launching and leading organization alignment. They report on misalignments within their divisions and ensure new processes, structures, or other practices are funded or existing ones adjusted to produce the strategic capabilities required by the business.

Remember that organization alignment happens every day anyway. People are always finding new ways to get work done and creating new practices and policies to make things easier and better. But generally they collaborate in small groups, which can get out of sync with the whole.

Continual, systemic alignment assessments are needed both to identify and amplify small pockets of innovation and to tune up the whole enterprise.

Syncing these assessments with the business planning cycle ensures that resources will get dedicated to correcting misalignments with the highest priority.

Summary: Imperfect Flexibility

The ability to continuously remold itself is one of the most important capabilities an organization can develop. Developing a systemic deftness at identifying misalignments and then mobilizing to correct them reduces the otherwise arduous resistance of people who do not do this work very often and are not aware how surgical it can be.

The biologist and naturalist Edward O. Wilson reminds us about the good news of incessant organization change. "Human beings and their social orders are intrinsically imperfectible," he says, "and fortunately so. In a constantly changing world, we need the flexibility that only imperfection provides."[2]

Key Organization Alignment Concepts

Thinking about an ongoing cadence of organization renewal offers two more concepts for our list:

- Regularly review the organization's performance vis-à-vis the evolving marketplace as part of your business or operational planning cadence.

- Recognize that no organization design is perfect; don't hesitate to make changes as soon as it is clear that an organizing choice is not working well.

What You Can Do Now

You can assess your organization periodically for its fitness to the marketplace. If this is not yet a formal, periodic process in your company, your change partner can help. He can suggest diagnostic methods, and he can help you integrate organization alignment into your business planning process.

At the end of each chapter, you have been reflecting on a specific organization design challenge. For this last reflection, consider your overall organization. Respond to the following questions about continuous organization alignment.

	Alignment leader responses	Change partner responses
What mechanisms exist to help us identify and react to marketplace changes and business opportunities?		
How do we improve discussions around needed organization changes in the context of marketplace, competitive and strategic shifts?		
How well does our business planning process support the alignment of organizing choices?		
How do we know when a specific organizing choice drifts far enough out of alignment that action should be taken?		
What does our leadership development program offer to help build organization alignment skills?		

MASTERING THE CUBE

At the beginning of the book, we explained how organizations are like Rubik's Cubes. You can't change one face without affecting all the others, and there's no going back once you make a move. Erno Rubik himself, twisting his new invention for the first time, found that he could not easily get all the colored blocks back to their correct sides. He toyed with it for over a month before he discovered certain routines that enabled him to reliably return the cube to order.[1]

The 8 Building Blocks we've set up for you in the preceding chapters are a little bit like these routines. By using them as stepping stones, you can become a confident organization aligner. They are techniques that will help you master the complexity of designing and implementing networks of organizing choices to produce the strategic capabilities required by your marketplace approach.

Alignment Leadership

As Harvard Business School professor and author Clayton Christensen has taught, successful companies will get pushed aside if they do not hearken to the threat of disruptive innovations and adjust their strategies in response. We would emphasize that *strategic change is not what's hard. What's really hard is organizational change to accommodate strategic change.* Processes, structures, measures, information systems, people systems, continuous improvement protocols, and cultural beliefs all must coalesce around a new strategic idea, or it will never deliver the desired results.

"A surprising number of innovations fail not because of some fatal technological flaw or because the market isn't ready," writes Christensen and co-author Raynor in their book *The Innovator's Solution*. "They fail because responsibility to build these businesses is given to managers or organizations whose capabilities aren't up to the task. Corporate executives make this mistake because most often the very skills that propel an organization to succeed in sustaining circumstances systematically bungle the best ideas for disruptive growth. An organization's *capabilities* become its *disabilities* when disruption is afoot."[2] The capabilities that have brought firms laurels in the past will sabotage them in the future if they cannot supplement them or replace them with new sets of organizing choices that produce fresh new capabilities.

You do not want to be that guy—the manager whose "capabilities aren't up to the task." Rather, as an alignment leader you want to be a systems thinker, continually monitoring the effectiveness of strategies, processes, structures, and other organizing choices. You want to be confident in detecting misalignments and astute in guiding realignments of either transformative or incremental scale. You want to be trusted to take on new strategic challenges because you possess the know-how to put a capable organization together.

Any changes you make can have far-reaching, long-lasting consequences, both intended and unintended. So proceed wisely. Done well, organization realignment can change the way a business goes to market, how leaders think, and how employees engage.

Change Partnering

Remember that you do not have to do this work alone. This book has described some of the most important building blocks for leading organization alignment. But you do not have to be an expert hands-on practitioner yourself. In fact, as we explained in discussing Stumbling

Block 3: The Secret Society, determining and designing new organization capabilities is most effective when it is an interactive process. Leadership groups need to jointly articulate their value propositions, struggle together to define trade-offs, and haggle over what work in the organization is and is not of the greatest marketplace value. It is in these difficult but exhilarating discussions that thinking changes and harmonizes at the leadership level. Because as a leader you need to be in the middle of this fray, you should feel the strong support of a change partner who can chart a road map for any scale of alignment, facilitate discussions, and provide tools for moving firmly and rapidly to build out capabilities across all the six sides of the organizational cube.

Change partners with these skills may come from human resources, organization design/effectiveness, change management, strategy, information technology, or process/continuous improvement. We hope you have had the opportunity to do as we suggested at the beginning of this book—to identify an alignment problem in your current organization, discuss it with a trusted change partner, and share your insights about each stumbling and building block. If not, find a change partner now and engage with her or him about these topics. (And if you are a change partner, please engage the leaders in your organization in alignment work and thinking. Reading this book together is a great place to start.)

Over the years, we have helped thousands of change partners learn the tools and approaches of organization alignment as well as deepen their experience and confidence in working alongside executives in the alignment process. Change partners need a clear set of concepts and language for talking to executives about organization alignment. We have shared these concepts in this book. In addition, a robust set of methodologies and tools can provide a way forward that leaders and their partners can both put their trust in so as to set forth confidently together. To learn more about specific methods and tools for leading alignment efforts, please visit masteringthecube.com.

Key Organization Alignment Concepts Consolidated

As we discussed, each building block in the prior chapters also suggested a series of organization alignment concepts or principles. Now we bring these together, slightly reorganized, for your reference and discussion with your change partner.

Figure 9.1: Leading Organization Alignment

Organization Alignment Methodology

The first set of concepts covers characteristics of a good alignment methodology itself—a good routine for diagnosing, planning, and executing alignment initiatives. You and your change partner can bear these in mind when talking about how to proceed with alignment work.

- Regularly review the organization's performance vis-à-vis the evolving marketplace as part of your business or operational planning cadence. (Building Block 8: Design Fluidly)

- Use an alignment process that has a clear road map from strategy and its trade-offs through capabilities to organization choices. (Building Block 3: Co-create)

- Use an organization alignment model to help you consider the full range of organizing choices, including work processes, structure, and other management systems. Remember that structure is just one aspect of a successful organization architecture. (Building Block 1: Align All Systems)

- Cascade organization alignment work down through the organization at a minimum of two levels of scope and detail. Macro (business model) alignment has the broadest scope and generates change in the business model and divisional/functional structures; micro (operational) alignment is more focused and brings about detailed change in processes, work groups, measurement systems, and people practices. (Building Block 5: Become an Alignment Leader)

- Recognize that no organization design is perfect; don't hesitate to make changes as soon as it is clear that an organizing choice is not working well. (Building Block 8: Design Fluidly)

Strategy

These concepts relate to the first step of alignment, which is to validate or resolve strategy. Remember that alignment is impossible without a clear strategy.

- Articulate the strategy, including trade-offs: state what unique value *will* be offered and what value *will not* be offered. (Building Block 1: Align All Systems). This is critical to minimize organization complexity for employees. (Building Block 7: Absorb Complexity)

- Unite the organization around a clear and targeted customer experience. (Building Block 7: Absorb Complexity)

- Lay out the strategic capabilities required by the organization to successfully implement the strategy and its accompanying trade-offs. (Building Block 1: Align All Systems)

- When your strategy is moving toward delivering ever more complex solutions, build new strategic capabilities for integration and linking. (Building Block 7: Absorb Complexity)

- Before building an organization that can deliver a complex customer solution strategy, be sure you understand the costs—both literal and organizational—of building the capabilities necessary to absorb complexity. It is going to be a lot of work and take a lot of time. (Building Block 7: Absorb Complexity)

Macro Alignment (Business Model Alignment)

The principles in this section are particularly relevant for leaders engaged in alignment of the highest process and structural levels of the organization. At a minimum, alignment activities at this level explore the business model, cultural behaviors that are strategically essential, the organization structure, linkages, high-level decision rights, and executive staffing.

- Imagine new and unique ways of doing work in the organization that will deliver differentiation in the marketplace. (Building Block 1: Align All Systems)

- Develop a tailored organizing option that fits your strategy and the trade-offs you are willing to make. (Building Block 2: Tailor to Strategy)

- Identify the downsides of the organizing option you have chosen. (Building Block 2: Tailor to Strategy)

- Don't copy competitors. (Building Block 2: Tailor to Strategy)

- Group work and people into divisions, teams, departments, and jobs that clearly define their impact on the strategy and the creation or enhancement of differentiating capabilities. (Building Block 1: Align All Systems)

- Protect strategically vital work from becoming engulfed by the transactional work that characterizes so much of what must get done on a daily basis. (Building Block 6: Resource *and* Reduce)

- Consider the strategic impact of work when making resourcing decisions. As a rule, generously allocate resources to strategic work with a goal of greater effectiveness, but manage non-competitive work toward greater efficiency. (Building Block 6: Resource *and* Reduce)

- Guard against functional imperatives and professional standards that are misaligned to strategy and don't enable differentiation or compliance. (Building Block 6: Resource *and* Reduce)

- Think through ways of linking people whose work is interdependent across boundaries to avoid or mitigate the downsides inherent in your structure. (Building Block 2: Tailor to Strategy)

- Understand and address the touch points between the capabilities you are building to overcome complexity. Think through ways of linking people whose work is interdependent across boundaries. (Building Block 7: Absorb Complexity)

- Clarify decision rights to accomplish what needs to be accomplished with the least confusion about who is responsible for what. (Building Block 1: Align All Systems)

- Identify cultural elements such as values and norms that are strategically important. Scrutinize leadership behaviors to ensure they reinforce espoused cultural beliefs. (Building Block 1: Align All Systems)

- Staff new jobs and jobs that change significantly because of the alignment *after* they have been designed. (Building Block 4: Staffing Follows Structure)

- Engage the leadership of the organization in the macro design process. In the end, they will be the ones to implement the new organization and adjust to the trade-offs. (Building Block 5: Become an Alignment Leader)

Micro Alignment (Operational Alignment)

These concepts come into play primarily in detailed alignment work, when teams of directors, managers, and subject matter experts redesign work processes; carry structure change to the bottom of the organization chart; determine new, aligned metrics; evaluate information systems; identify misalignments in people and reward systems; and institute or adjust continuous improvement practices. As an alignment leader, you should espouse them when your people are in the thick of alignment transformations, incorporating them into alignment team charters and relying on them to evaluate implementation plans.

- Redesign existing business processes, because if the work in an organization does not change, not much will change in marketplace results. (Building Block 1: Align All Systems)

- Design metrics to drive the desired outcomes and behaviors. (Building Block 1: Align All Systems)

- Prioritize technology investments with a clear sense of the strategic impact. (Building Block 1: Align All Systems)

- Revamp people selection processes, employee development practices, performance management systems, and reward systems if necessary to align with the ultimate aims. (Building Block 1: Align All Systems)

- Consider habits regarding organization learning, ensuring that you continually review and improve performance. (Building Block 1: Align All Systems)

- Consider how all organizing choices will contribute to greater integration, including work processes, decision making, structure, metrics, and other management systems. (Building Block 7: Absorb Complexity)

- Engage those who do the work of the organization in the micro design process. In the end, they will be the ones who must do the work differently from before. (Building Block 5: Become an Alignment Leader)

Change Management

These are change management principles. We only skirted the broad topic of change management in our book, but the principles below are so essential we could not have a complete discussion of alignment without delving into them.

- Involve many people in the organization in planning and implementing the alignment to get the best thinking—and to change thinking—throughout the ranks. (Besides, it will accelerate the time implement!) (Building Block 3: Co-create)

- Incorporate change management practices and tools into the organizational alignment methodology from its earliest stages. (Building Block 3: Co-create)

Change Leadership

The principles in this group are about alignment leadership specifically: they apply to you and your team.

- Build internal alignment leadership capability for creating organization alignment and managing change that really takes hold. (Building Block 5: Become an Alignment Leader)
- Ensure leadership involvement is broad and remains committed to sponsoring a significant organization alignment effort from planning and chartering through full implementation. (Building Block 5: Become an Alignment Leader)

Alignment Aphorisms

Here is a catalog of the sayings that we meted out throughout the book to emphasize some of the main points of each chapter. (These are marked with black arrows.)

Building Block 1: Align All Systems

- Strategic alignment demands strategic trade-offs.
- Strategy is about the future; capabilities are about the past.
- Understanding the delta between your current capabilities and the needed capabilities is the crux of organization alignment.
- If the work doesn't change, results don't change.
- Differentiating activities deliver competitive differentiation.
- Your ability to compete lies in the activities you choose to do and how you choose to resource them.
- Strategy drives work. Work drives structure.
- Alignment leaders are alignment-minded.
- Differentiation is by design.

Building Block 2: Tailor to Strategy

- Saying yes to a customer you should have said no to means saying no to a customer you should have said yes to.

- Linkages trump structure.

Building Block 3: Co-create

- You cannot achieve different results without helping people learn how to think differently.

- To be dubbed organization aligners for a few weeks converts people into alignment leaders for the rest of their careers.

Building Block 4: Staffing Follows Structure

- Talent by itself can't deliver strategy.

Building Block 5: Become an Alignment Leader

- Alignment leaders are passionate about optimal organization alignment to strategy.

- Organization alignment efforts are not complete until micro alignment choices are put into action.

Building Block 6: Resource and Reduce

- Spending where you shouldn't prevents you from investing where you should.

Building Block 7: Absorb Complexity

- If you hope to become a complexity sponge for your clients, you must develop new complexity-absorbing capabilities.

- Simplicity for the customer first; simplicity for the organization second.

Building Block 8: Design Fluidly

- The set of upsides and downsides that characterize your organization have an expiration date.

- Continual, systemic alignment assessments are needed both to identify and amplify small pockets of innovation and to tune up the whole enterprise.

The Wild Beast

The architect who inspired the integrating metaphor for this book said of his own invention:

> In its arranged state [the Rubik's Cube] suggests calm, peace, a sense of order, security . . . in sharp contrast to all that the working object means once it is brought to life, to motion. There is something terrifying in its calm state, like a wild beast at rest, a tiger in repose, its power lurking.[3]

Organizations of any size, of course, can never be brought to an arranged state that is perfect. Perhaps this takes a little terror out of the responsibility of the job. Organizations are always in some disarray, powerful tigers on the prowl.

May you fare well as you change, prosper, and protect yours from extinction.

Notes

Alignment and the Multifaceted Organization

1. John Tierney, "The Perplexing Life of Erno Rubik," *Discover*, March 1986, 81, as reprinted at http://www.puzzlesolver.com/puzzle.php?id=29;page=15.

2. Michael D. Watkins, "How Managers Become Leaders: The Seven Seismic Shifts of Perspective and Responsibility," *Harvard Business Review*, June 2012, 69.

3. Ibid.

Chapter 1

1. Brad Stone, *The Everything Store: Jeff Bezos and the Age of Amazon* (New York: Little, Brown, and Company, 2013), 171.

2. Ibid., 173.

3. Starbucks, "Starbucks Strengthens Leadership Team," news release, January 29, 2014, http://news.starbucks.com/news/starbucks-strengthens-senior-leadership-team; see also "Leadership Team," starbucks.com, accessed February 5, 2014, http://news.starbucks.com/leadership.

4. "Starbucks Strengthens Leadership Team."

5. "Michael Conway: Executive Vice President, Global Channel Development," Starbucks.com, accessed February 5, 2014, http://news.starbucks.com/leadership/michael-conway.

6. Chris Murphy, "Starbucks' Stephen Gillett: InformationWeek's IT Chief of the Year," informationweek.com, December 2, 2011, accessed February 5, 2014, http://www.informationweek.com/it-leadership/starbucks-stephen-gillett-information-weeks-it-chief-of-the-year-/d/d-id/1101620; Darell Etterington, "Mobile Payment at U.S. Starbucks Locations Crosses 10% as More Stores Get Wireless Charging," techcrunch.com, July 26, 2013, http://techcrunch.com/2013/07/26/mobile-payment-at-u-s-starbucks-locations-crosses-10-as-more-stores-get-wireless-charging.

7. Howard Shultz with Joanne Gordon, *Onward: How Starbucks Fought for Its Life without Losing Its Soul* (New York: Rodale, 2011), 90; see also "Starbucks' Quest for Healthy Growth: An Interview with Howard Shultz," *The McKinsey Quarterly*, March 2011, McKinsey.com, accessed February 5, 2014, http://www.mckinsey.com/insights/growth/starbucks_quest_for_healthy_growth_an_interview_with_howard_schultz.

8. Ibid.

9. See, for example, Adi Ignatius, interview with Howard Shultz, "We Had to Own the Mistakes," *Harvard Business Review*, March 2011, 112.

10. Elaine Wong, "Starbucks Is the Top Brand on Facebook," *AdWeek*, August 12, 2009, adweek.com, accessed February 5, 2014, http://www.adweek.com/news/advertising-branding/why-starbucks-top-brand-facebook-106237.

11. Stone, *Everything Store*, 75, 87–88, 330.

12. Ignatius, "We Had to Own the Mistakes," 111–12.

13. Bernd Heinrich, *Why We Run: A Natural History* (New York: Ecco, 2001), Kindle edition.

14. Ibid.

15. Ibid.

Chapter 2

1. Voluntary turnover at Starbucks was 9 percent in 2013. See "100 Best Companies to Work For: Starbucks," money.cnn.com, accessed February 4, 2014, http://money.cnn.com/magazines/fortune/best-companies/2013/snapshots/94.html?iid=bc_lp_arrow1. This compares to a casual dining industry rate of 44 percent. See Linda Ray, "Employee Turnover Statistics in Restaurants," *Houston Chronicle*, chron.com, accessed February 4, 2014, http://smallbusiness.chron.com/employee-turnover-statistics-restaurants-16744.html.

2. Starbucks, "Starbucks Appoints Head of Global Human Resources," news release, October 29, 2009, http://investor.starbucks.com/phoenix.zhtml?c=99518&p=irol-newsArticle&ID=1348692&highlight=.

3. "The Seed of Apple's Innovation," *BusinessWeek*, October 12, 1994, quoted in Alan Siegel and Irene Etzkorn, *Simple: Conquering the Crisis of Complexity* (New York: Twelve, 2013), 155.

4. Walter Isaacson, *Steve Jobs* (New York: Simon and Schuster, 2011), 21, 408. See Building Block 5: Become an Alignment Leader.

Chapter 3

1. See Jürgen Habermas, *The Theory of Communicative Action, Volume 1: Reason and the Rationalization of Society*, trans. Thomas McCarthy (Boston: Beacon Press, 1981), 294.

Chapter 4

1. Jim Collins, *Good to Great* (New York: HarperCollins, 2001), 41; cf. 41–64.

Chapter 5

1. Isaacson, *Steve Jobs*, 128.

2. Ibid., 334.

3. Ibid., 359.

4. Ibid., 362.

5. Ibid.

6. Ibid., 362–63.

7. Ibid., 346.

8. Ibid., 408.

9. Ibid., 336.

10. Ibid., 359.

11. Ibid., 333.

12. Ibid., 339.

13. Ibid., 359–61.

14. Ibid., 461.

Chapter 6

1. Ibid., 337.

2. Ibid., 378-79.

Chapter 7

1. Marty Neumeier, *Zag: The #1 Strategy of High-Performance Brands* (Berkeley: New Riders, 2007), 15.

2. Siegel and Etzkorn, *Simple: Conquering the Crisis of Complexity*, 32.

3. Ibid., 34.

4. B. Joseph Pine and James H. Gilmore, *The Experience Economy* (Boston: Harvard Business Review Press, 2011), 5.

5. As quoted in Stone, *Everything Store*, 38.

6. Ibid, 339.

7. Isaacson, *Steve Jobs*, 343.

8. Anders Dahvig, *The Ikea Edge: Building Global Growth and Social Good at the World's Most Iconic Home Store* (New York: McGraw Hill, 2012), 71.

Chapter 8

1. Pine and Gilmore, *Experience Economy*.

2. Edward O. Wilson, *The Social Conquest of Earth* (New York: Liveright, 2012), 241.

Mastering the Cube

1. Tierney, "Perplexing Life of Erno Rubik."

2. Clayton M. Christensen and Michael E. Raynor, *The Innovator's Solution* (Boston: Harvard Business School Press, 2003), 177.

3. Tierney "Perplexing Life of Erno Rubik."

About the Authors

Reed Deshler is a principal with AlignOrg Solutions and a leading organization design and change practice leader with extensive corporate and consulting experience. He has worked with leaders at some of the largest and most respected companies in the world. Leaders appreciate Reed's expertise in the science of organization design and change coupled with how he artfully diagnoses organization misalignments and facilitates the insights needed to drive business change and growth. Reed is a regular presenter at industry conferences and is a noted educator of organization design and change management skills with business executives around the world.

Kreig Smith is the founder of AlignOrg Solutions and a principal with the firm. He has consulted with a wide range of organizations—from Fortune 50 corporations to small businesses, for profit and nonprofit organizations, and domestic and international enterprises—for nearly thirty years. His expertise centers in the alignment of organizations to marketplace positions. Kreig focuses on large-scale change efforts, strategy clarification, organization design, and education. A presenter at many national and international conferences on organization design and change, Kreig is also a certified GE Crotonville instructor.

Alyson Von Feldt guides major organization design initiatives with AlignOrg Solutions at enterprises ranging from startups to Fortune 50 companies. With a background in both the profit and nonprofit sectors, Alyson has led business unit design teams charged with aligning structures, workflows, and systems to strategy. As a writer, she develops robust tools and training programs that showcase and simplify powerful design techniques, and she documents the stories of intriguing high-performing organizations. Alyson is an author of *Running into the Wind: 5 Strategies for Building a Successful Team*.

AlignOrg Solutions is an international consultancy serving enterprises of all sizes and types to clarify strategy, align organizational choices, build organization capabilities, manage and implement change, and develop alignment leadership. The firm offers a high-engagement approach, exceptional alignment tools, and hard-won expertise in leading organization transformation projects. They are respected worldwide for helping leaders and their change partners align the choices in their organizations with a differentiated strategy for future success.

To learn more, please visit masteringthecube.com.

Made in the USA
Las Vegas, NV
18 October 2023

79302424R00096